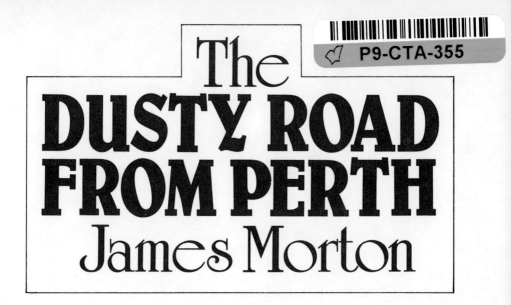

The DUSTY ROAD FROM PERTH

James Morton

DOUGLÁS & McINTYRE

Vancouver/Toronto

Douglas & McIntyre Ltd.
1615 Venables Street
Vancouver, British Columbia

Canadian Cataloguing in Publication Data

Morton, James, 1922–
    The dusty road from Perth

    ISBN 0-88894-321-0

    1. Morton family.   2. Morton, James, 1922–
    3. Scots in Canada.   I. Title.
    CS90.M67 1981   929'.2   C81-091270-8

Jacket design by Nancy Legue
Printed and bound in Canada by John Deyell Company

For
Maymie Padkin Lindsay

prologue

My father was not a warrior, a politician or a mogul of the business world. In his day he was well known by his professional colleagues, marginally by the public and superficially by his children. No streets, buildings or parks were named after him. Yet glancing back at him from a greatly changed social world, through the filter of two decades, he was a remarkable man. He was accepted merely as a father in the world of the present by his children, who knew little of his recent past and nothing of his more distant origins—and did not particularly care. He lived in a tight little community dominated by Scots, all of whom were deeply attached to their homeland, though few would live to see it again. His origins, five thousand miles away, were inaccessible to him for most of his life, yet a changing world allowed his children and his grandchildren not only to see them but also to experience them. One's roots are there for anyone who is sufficiently curious to see and to experience, whether his name is the same as my father's or not. He was not squeezed from a tube into Burnaby in 1912, like a figure on a wedding cake. Do you wish to be no more than a dog—who is friendly, faithful and intelligent but who does not care who his mother and father were? Do you ever wonder why you were one of those select few who were spared? Do you realize that your direct ancestors survived the Black Plague and the lances and arrows of one side or the other—indeed all the plagues and wars that have beset mankind since the beginning of time? My father's ancestors survived and, through centuries of alliances, produced a man who was different from anyone the world had ever known. And the product was a good one.

one

There is a vast expanse in both time and space between the ragged tramp of Prince Charles's followers upon the North Inch and the rattle of my father's McLaughlin Buick on Fourteenth Avenue, yet that is where my world began and ended. Five thousand miles and two hundred years. Indeed, if records were available, one could retreat to the very beginning of time, yet two centuries is a respectable age for the family tree of the tenants of the Gallowmuir and Muirton farms.

Those early forebears of my father certainly would have heard of the strange assemblage of highland clans exercising awkwardly a few miles north of the Gallowmuir, and surely they raised their eyes from the soil long enough to contemplate Charles Edward Stewart and his proud and confident army tramping down the dusty road from Perth. Perhaps they were unsympathetic to the Stewart cause, there on the fertile soil below the rolling hills to the north, but they would be familiar with Charles's exploits, just as they soon would be familiar with the exploits of Washington, Wellington and Napoleon. Perhaps they were less familiar with the great literary, musical and artistic figures of the day—Johnson and Boswell, Reynolds, Garrick, Goldsmith, Sheridan, Burke, Gibbon, Hogarth, Ramsay, Raeburn, Handel, Haydn, or the magnificent Vivaldi who had died shortly before the royal tartan of Charles Edward Stewart, resplendent in the warm September sun in

1745, marched southward on the crusade which came within an eyelash of changing the destiny of England and Scotland. Perhaps they glanced up only momentarily. Wheat and barley and neeps were more important than poets and warriors.

Had John Morton laid down his plough and his hoe that early September morning, he might have died in the field of battle, and neither I nor my children would exist. The ragged army, torn by clannish dissension, was butchered on the dismal moors of Culloden in April of the following year. But John did not lay down his plough and his hoe. He turned again to the soil and howked his neeps and I looked up and saw the square, strong hands of my father grasping the smooth wooden steering wheel of the McLaughlin Buick as it bounced over the potholes of Fourteenth Avenue five thousand miles and two centuries from the North Inch, from Gallowmuir and the artistic geniuses of the eighteenth century. It was so distant in the past that my father had never heard of the Gallowmuir— and to me there was no past. I saw my father's hands grasping the wooden steering wheel, or grasping a saw as he patiently assembled the rustic fence about his garden, or grasping a heavy hammer as he split the great granite rocks to build the pillars at the foot of the driveway. My father had always performed these tasks. There had been no one before him. There was no John Morton, no Gallowmuir and certainly no Charles Edward Stewart marching southward to his dismal destiny. My father had always been thirty years of age. There was no past—nor, for that matter, no future. There was just present.

And yet a past, at some point, came imperceptibly into existence. At first it had no shape or form. It was not a mass of historical facts presented academically or chronologically; it was a series of isolated and unrelated words or phrases or perhaps sentences—a comment dropped casually by a parent, the nostalgic reminiscences of friends, or occasionally a personal story designed to amuse a child. They were merely little flecks of information, many of them entering the childish mind subliminally, to be recollected at some distant future date, to be combined with newly discovered facts that form a past which we all possess, a past of no interest to some but of immeasurable interest to others.

My sister, my brother and I slowly became aware that our parents were Scottish, that our father had been born on or near a farm in Perth, that he had a mother and a brother in Scotland, and that his father had died when he was very young. We knew that he had been in World War I, for on the dull, listless days of childhood we would amuse ourselves by dressing in his tunic, helmet and gas mask which hung on a nail in the darkest recess of our attic. But our father spoke little of the past. Occasionally he would amuse us with a fascinating adventure from his childhood days on the Muirton Farm, the exact location, the size and the ownership of which were all very vague in our young minds. Or he would tell us how he rebuilt a boat and rowed up the River Tay to the Sawmill Stream, or how he raced down Lochy Brae on his bicycle in search of a doctor to save his maternal grandfather who ultimately died of a burst aorta. But they were isolated tales which did not reflect his daily life, his schooling, his relations with his mother, brother and uncles, or indicate whether he had an unhappy childhood or an impoverished youth. Our father, like his children, lived in the present.

Our mother, on the other hand, lived to a great extent in the happy memories of her past. We knew every detail of her life with the exception, we later learned, of those delicate but innocent situations that she considered might embarrass her children or herself. We knew that her mother had died in 1918 of a strange disease called pernicious anaemia. We knew that her father still lived in Perth. We knew the names of all her brothers and sisters and their children as well as the names of all her friends and that they were all kind, loving, honest—nay—saintly individuals. We knew the streets of her beloved Perth, the playing fields of the North Inch, the musicals in

which she sang as a young woman, where she walked on a
Sunday after the service in the North Church—and we knew of
the anguish she suffered when she left her home after the war.
She carried on a regular correspondence with numerous relatives and friends. Our father never did. Our mother lived in
the recollections of the past, our father in the reality of the
present.

It was only reasonable, then, to conclude that our parents
arrived in the west in 1919, but it is reasonable only because
our mother would frequently remind us of the exact date on
which *she* arrived in Canada and the exact date on which she
arrived in Burnaby. It was, however, an incorrect conclusion;
our father paid no attention to past memorable events, including the date of his arrival in the west, which old photographs
later proved to be 1912. But why did he leave his native land?
He was not driven out by vengeful Englishmen, as were the
Highlanders following the calamity at Culloden. Why did he
leave his mother and brother and countless uncles and his
beloved Muirton Farm to become a civil engineer in a wilderness five thousand miles away? How, indeed, did a fatherless
child with a heritage of two centuries of farming become an
engineer? Certainly he attended Sharpe's Institution in Perth
since my mother, in her nostalgic ramblings, described him in
her sister's class. And certainly he spoke of Perth Academy, on
the edge of the North Inch. An old photograph filed away in
the lower right-hand drawer of his ancient roll-top desk was
perhaps the only clue. It still exists, as it did in my childhood.
Twenty-nine students, eighteen of whom are women, are
dressed in academic gowns, and on the reverse, in my father's
hand, is the legend, "University College, University of St.
Andrews, 1905-1906." In the upper right-hand corner stands a
handsome seventeen-year-old—my father.

Six years later he stood on the outside steps of a little cottage
on Ulster Street in Burnaby to have his photograph taken.
What could have happened in that short period? To his chil-

dren it was past history and of no interest—nor, perhaps, to him. Yet he preserved a letter dated 12 September 1912, possibly out of sentiment or a sense of history, or perhaps because he recognized that it represented a turning point in his life—or perhaps the letter merely fell accidentally amongst other more important papers. It was an offer of a job from the Dominion Department of Public Works in New Westminster. "The situation" was a temporary one at a salary of one hundred dollars a month. "It must be distinctly understood," the letter emphasized, "that your appointment is during the pleasure of the department." It was signed "C. C. Worsfold, District Engineer." To my father's children, that awesome name became a symbol of respect, authority and fear, to say nothing of security.

Seven years later my father returned to Burnaby from World War I with his bride, my mother. But this was the past to their children, who knew only that their parents had first lived on Ulster Street in a cottage named Lingannoch. I knew this much since it was said that my sister was born while our parents lived there. I can also recall visiting the house one Saturday afternoon when it was unoccupied, and once, in the dark days of the Depression, I overheard the tenant, Mrs. Currie, inform my mother in a calm and dignified manner that she would be unable to pay the twelve dollars' rent for that month.

The Ulster Street cottage was a mile closer to Vancouver than the new house my father built on Fourteenth Avenue in 1922, the year of my birth. Although my mother's three confinements took place in St. Mary's in New Westminster—Burnaby, after all, was far too poor and sparsely populated to enjoy the luxury of a hospital—we three children spent our lives up to adulthood in that Fourteenth Avenue home. It was an historical site as far as our little corner of the world was concerned, since it was just off Douglas Road (now Canada Way), the original trail to Burrard Inlet long before the Cana-

dian Pacific Railway invented Vancouver. And the other thoroughfare to the sea, the False Creek Trail, branched off
precisely at Fourteenth, presumably cutting over my father's
property. But this would have been of no interest to him, had
he known, though it might have tickled his fancy just a trifle if
he had realized that a gentleman named John Morton had
walked over that trail sixty years earlier to preempt the site of
the future West End of Vancouver. My father had a brother
and an uncle, as well as many other antecedents stretching back
to the early eighteenth century, with exactly the same name.
However, the John Morton of the West End—unfortunately,
by my father's standards—was an Englishman and hardly worthy of walking across my father's property.

It was in this house, set upon two lots, that my father settled
at the age of thirty years and it was here that he raised his
family. To his children this was the world. Perth was in a
magic land a million miles away, a land we were not at all sure
even existed. The world was Burnaby—or, more accurately,
South Burnaby—or still more accurately, the world was Fourteenth Avenue and Burgess Street and Douglas Road and, to a
lesser extent, New Westminster. The border of the town was
only four blocks down the hill, and the very heart of that
shabby metropolis—if indeed Columbia Street could be termed
a street and New Westminster a metropolis—was just two
miles to the south. Its old brick and wooden buildings stretched
untidily for about half a mile up Columbia Street from Eighth
Street, ending somewhat abruptly between the Columbia Theatre and the City Market. It was just a little strip of town two
blocks deep. Columbia Street, with its double row of streetcar
tracks and a single line of metal poles between them, was its
spine. There was nothing else.

New Westminster was the city, though one who happened
accidentally to stumble into it on the road north to Vancouver
might well have questioned this. Yet to the Giffords, the
Bewses, the Burrs, the Trapps, the Baxters and the Collisters,
who owned the main establishments on Columbia Street, New

Westminster was a great metropolis and they were its greatest citizens. Mr. Woolworth, who owned a fifteen-cent store on the same street, must be excluded from this group of distinguished citizens since he never, to my knowledge, put in an appearance.

The city slept peacefully beside the Fraser River from Sunday morning until dawn on Friday when the farmers from the valley poured in across the old railway bridge to sell their fruit and vegetables, their cows and horses, their cats and dogs and, in some instances, their needlework and crochet. Every housewife for miles around ambled casually up Columbia Street to the City Market, perched high on the bank above the river— and plodded down again, their shoulders swaying beneath the weight of their bulging baskets. Both sides of the street were a solid mass of housewives until noon on Friday, at which time there was a lull that lasted until Saturday afternoon and evening when the country folk from across the river came to shop. From Newton and Strawberry Hill, from Fry's Corner, Whalley's Corner, Cloverdale and maybe even from Langley. They were easily distinguished from the Giffords and Bewses, the Burrs and Trapps. The country folk from across the river shuffled uncertainly down Columbia Street, their weatherbeaten faces black against ill-fitting, white collars, their old-fashioned clothes falling loosely from their shoulders, their great black hands hanging awkwardly far below their sleeves. A stranger in town could not possibly mistake them for the dapper grandeur of Bill Gifford, dressed in his tailored blue serge suit with his clean-shaven face and blond, wavy hair. Nor for Walter Nixon who bustled around so confidently in his grey pin-stripe, his arms swinging briskly, as if the future of the whole business community depended upon him. And George Cassidy? Why he was so tall and white-haired and smiling, and he loped down Columbia Street with such long, relaxed strides, that absolutely no one could possibly mistake him for one of the country folk from across the river.

It was very rural over there. Our side of the river above

New Westminster was, perhaps, semirural. Carpenters, plasterers, mill workers and assorted day labourers lived there in shingle or stucco houses. The head of each family would set off early in the morning, carrying his lunch pail, for the streetcar on Sixth Street or Kingsway, and return again late in the afternoon. Few of our neighbours had cars, and perhaps it was a blessing, for, though Fourteenth Avenue was roughly paved with asphalt, the springs and tires of our McLaughlin Buick suffered considerably from the potholes. The side roads off Fourteenth were all dirt, and no matter on what class of road you lived—paved or unpaved, potholed or not potholed—there were deep ditches on both sides into which drained the septic tanks of every house on the street. The brush on the boulevards was lush. It was really quite a depressed district in the economic sense, though there were also magnificent stretches of timber and bushes and fields. Just past the three houses on the lower part of Burgess Street you could plunge into a bushland of alders and willows and hazels, and great rotting stumps of ancient firs and cedars where squirrels hid their hazelnuts. In the spring you could walk there beneath the trees and hear last year's bracken snap beneath your feet and you could see the sticky heads of ferns unfolding from the ground and, in the damp hollows, white and pink trilliums.

There was bush right across from us on Fourteenth and another great sweep of bush between our house and Douglas Road, extending all the way around to Mrs. Crawford's chicken house. And right across Burgess was a field where apple trees grew and where Mr. Chilton chained his goat to an iron spike. Just about everyone in our neighbourhood had goats or chickens or cows. As a matter of fact, we always got our milk from Mr. Whittaker who kept about a dozen cows—Nan, Nifty, Nellie, Nola—just up the lane off Burgess. We had to go for it ourselves. You would start by hunting for the scissors in our kitchen, often the most time-consuming part of the whole procedure. You needed the scissors to cut off one of the rectangular tickets outlined in pencil on a piece of stiff green paper which Mrs. Whittaker provided for her customers and which you placed in the neck of the bottle. You put on your raincoat, since it always seemed to be raining when you went for the milk, and you wandered out the back gate and up the lane. There were hazards in that lane, for the cows used it as a thoroughfare, but the greatest was the wet, slippery planks laid across Whittaker's back garden. My mother did not appreciate a broken bottle or a lost quart of milk, though she always commended us for retrieving the green ticket. Sometimes you had to fill the bottle yourself from a bucket in the dairy and walk home with it warm in your hands. No one ever worried about germs—and anyway, my father did not believe in them since he could not see them.

Mr. Whittaker used to drive those cows, mooing and messing up the street, down Burgess, along Fourteenth and down Hilda Street to the field on Twelfth Avenue, or sometimes to Gillespie's Field behind his house, or up Burgess past Mrs. Stewart's house—where there was a mysterious well covered with a shingled, gabled roof—to yet another field. And directly behind us, Mrs. Crawford had a huge hen house, and on the other side of her, Eulice Dowd raised chickens by the thousands. When you went there to buy a dozen eggs, Eulice would show you his incubator and the little light he used to examine whether an egg was fertile or not, though at the time I did not know what this meant. Or he might raise a chicken's rump to show you an egg emerging. Just about everyone had chickens. Mrs. Edmonston along Fourteenth had a great batch of them and Mr. Holt had a few behind his gas station on the corner and even my friend Corkie had some Bantams which produced lovely little brown eggs. Burnaby, of which I am a patriot, was indeed a semirural district. In retrospect, it was quite unlike the outskirts of Perth where my father had lived. New Westminster, on the other hand, though smaller, was similar in the sense that it was the centre to which farmers came to shop or to stand on street corners and discuss the weather or the weighty farming problems of the day.

The folk across the river were foreigners, not because they lived across the river but rather because they spoke in strange tongues. The "Hindus" who came over from Queensborough were not included in this class. They were British and they spoke our language. But the others—you could hear them on Saturday nights on Columbia Street. It is entirely possible that only one in twenty was European, but this was quite enough to label them all foreigners and we were mightily suspicious of them. There were fewer of them on our side of the river. The bulk of our population was Canadian, but scattered widely throughout the community were a goodly number of Scots, amongst whom could proudly be numbered my parents. My mother, and to a less extent my father, could never forget that they were Scottish, that their home was still Perth. The High Street, Gannochy Road and the Dunkeld Road, and Methven Street and Tay Street, Lochy Brae, the North Inch, Kinnoull Hill—they were all just as familiar names to us as Fourteenth Avenue, Burgess Street and Douglas Road, and much more romantic. But to us, those days when our parents lived in Scotland were far off in the distant past. They were just as mysterious and just as ancient as the days of King Arthur and his Knights of the Round Table. When my memory began to form, my father had been in Canada for over fifteen years, with the exception of his service overseas. His love for Scotland had perhaps been blunted slightly by time, or perhaps it was his inclination to forget the past, but my mother had been away from home for a mere seven or eight years and her love for it was as strong as the day she departed.

Every Scottish parent in the community was the same. "Home" was Scotland, and they lived and breathed only for the day they could visit their homeland—just for a visit, mind you, just for a visit. In most instances it was a forlorn hope: there was little money, little job security, little holiday time, and travelling by train and by boat was very slow. The patriotic Scots of Burnaby could not visit their homeland, but this did not prevent them from discussing their dreams endlessly.

They made it worse, too, by herding together. There was seldom a soul who visited our home who was not Scottish. There were the Stuarts of Pitlochry, the McCullochs of Oban, the Robertsons of Aberdeen, the McCraes of Perth, the Gibsons of Glenboig, the Philpses of Hamilton and the Healys of Edinburgh—and a great many others. When an Englishman managed to find his way into our house, it was invariably through some relationship he or she had with a Scottish friend of ours. Take Mr. Webster, for instance. He was really Welsh, though anyone born below the border was, to my father, English. In spite of the misfortune of his birth, however, Mr. Webster was admitted to our home on a regular weekly basis. For some years this was a mystery to me, until I finally discovered that Mrs. Webster was a native of Kirkcudbright—which, of course, was a perfectly valid excuse for allowing her husband into our household.

Phyllis Saunders was another. Since she was not only Canadian but also of English parentage, the probability of her entering our front door was, to say the least, slim. Phyllis, however, was a close friend of the Ingrams and the Gregorys of Galashiels—or perhaps it was Melrose. It must have been Melrose, for I can remember Mrs. Gregory sitting on the great couch in our living room, looking at the new Scotsman Calendar, the arrival of which was always an important event in our home, and when she came to a photograph of Melrose Abbey, her eyes lit up and, in a voice rising and falling with emotion, she said, "I was bor-r-r-n there," and then, as an afterthought, ". . . but no' in the Awbbey!" The Ingrams and Gregorys, then, were Phyllis's key to our home.

There were hundreds of Scots about, and they kept cropping up in every imaginable place. One Sunday we drove out to Burquitlam in the new 1929 Nash my father had just purchased from Baxter Motors. Across from the golf course a new house was being built amongst the trees. Since it was not yet occupied, my father decided to inspect it. We had barely entered the door when the owner quite unexpectedly appeared. He expressed his displeasure in a polite but reserved manner—and in a fine Scottish drawl. "What part of Scotland are you from?" asked my father innocently. Even before the stranger could answer, his face had softened and there was immediate accord with my father and his family. The fact that the man was from Dundee, just down the Tay from Perth, did not matter. Anywhere north of the Tweed would have been perfectly satisfactory.

Then there was this miserable Scotch terrier at Bowen Island. Toby was his name. He would bark and snap at our heels—absolutely the most miserable beast that ever there was. And his owner was not much better; he would allow Toby to bark and snap to his heart's content. As it later developed, however, this fellow's name was MacBrayne; he was from the Island of Mull and his dog's proper name was Tobermory. It is remarkable what nice people they really were. Even Toby accepted us as friends after our breed had been established, without the formal submission of our pedigree.

Scots were the salt of the earth. And Englishmen? Well, you knew that they were clean and properly dressed, their speech was grammatically correct and their table manners were impeccable—but when you heard a well-cultivated Oxford accent, you just knew that you could not trust that person. When an Englishman did something that displeased my father, he knew no grosser insult than to growl disgustedly, "Typically English!"

Canadians did not fare much better as far as my father was concerned, though he at least did not distrust them; they were not smart enough to warrant distrust. Canadians, to my father, were people who did not wear neckties, people who did not speak grammatically, and people whose eating habits were most distasteful. If, for example, we used a double negative or the past instead of the present participle, my father would mutter in menacing tones, "We'll have none of that Canadian talk in this house!" Or if, in our adolescent desire to satisfy our hunger, we went about demolishing the evening meal too enthusiastically, he would angrily admonish the culprit with, "Don't put so much in your mouth. You're eating like a Canadian."

The unfortunate thing about this prejudice was that all his children were Canadians. Mind you, he always tried to circumvent the stigma by insisting that we were Scottish Canadians, but his children being half Canadian was a most annoying though unavoidable reality for my father. The only thing he could do, short of sending us to Scotland for an education, was to inculcate in us as many Scottish customs as he could, and this he did without, I am sure, being aware of it. It was a natural, completely unconscious result of his own upbringing and of the society in which we lived. We ate Scottish dishes prepared in the Scottish fashion and we handled our eating utensils in the prescribed Scottish manner. We were occasionlly regaled with tales of the Muirton Farm, rugby and cricket matches on the North Inch, walks upon Kinnoull Hill, pearls in the Tay and rowing up the Sawmill Stream. We were exposed to Scottish expressions and words, for which we knew most of the meanings but few of the spellings. How, for instance, does one spell "trauchled" or "bizzim"? "Bowfie" and "clartie" and "plouter" were not so difficult—but actually there was never any question of spelling them, and it is indeed entirely possible that our parents knew no more than we did in this regard.

We were always made aware of the truth that Canadian workmanship was shoddy whereas Scottish craftsmanship was beautiful, thorough and everlasting. And my father had a thing about brass. Canadians, he said, refused to manufacture brass; instead, they manufactured "cheap stuff" which would not last.

He would growl and grumble for weeks on end when he could not find a brass fitting for a piece of furniture he was making in his workshop, though I recall that on one occasion he did find a beautiful pair of brass hinges for the summerhouse which he built in the garden. His pleasure in discovering the real thing, however, was more than tempered by the excessive price he had to pay for it.

And there were Scottish morals—though it is perhaps inaccurate to term them Scottish. They were morals my father had been taught in Scotland. We were aware that there was an "English" church on Douglas Road up near Edmonds Street, but we, as children, gained the impression, rightly or wrongly, that it would have been sacrilege to enter it. I do not recall a Catholic church in our community, nor do I ever recall my father referring to Catholics, except on one occasion. He once returned from a business trip to Seattle to tell us, with considerable amusement, that on a Sunday morning he had gone down to the desk of the Washington Athletic Club and asked where the nearest church was. Now when my father inquired about a church, anyone with any sense would know perfectly well that he had a Presbyterian church in mind. To him, no others existed. The desk clerk, however, answered, "Why there's a Catholic church just around the corner, sir." To my very own father he said this. "That," answered my father, "is the last place I'd go to." Perhaps he said it in a jocular fashion, but he said it—and strode out in search of the only true church. That is the only time I ever heard him speak deprecatingly of another religion and I like to think he did so in jest.

Our family were members of the Gordon Presbyterian Church, which was as close to the Church of Scotland as you could get. My father was the superintendent of the Sunday School for more than thirty years as well as being an elder, a manager and a member of the choir. These activities not only served to expose his children to the moral standards he so desired but they also served to strengthen the bonds of the

Scottish community. There were perhaps a few Canadian members of the congregation, but in general, Canadians, in addition to their lack of neckties, their ungrammatical speech and their slovenly eating habits, were a godless lot. The Gordon Church was the rock upon which the Scottish community was built. There were Philpses, Taylors, Robertsons, Mathiesons, MacCraes, Grants, MacGillivrays, Mackenzies, Frasers and a great host of MacDonalds and MacLeods from Prince Edward Island and Nova Scotia—which were every bit as Scottish as Scotland.

Sunday was a trying day for my father's children. To begin with, he always prepared breakfast. On cold winter mornings he would mix the porridge. A pot of water would already be steaming on the coal and wood stove when we descended from our upstairs bedrooms. He would dip his hand into a large sack of rolled oats and let the grain trickle slowly through his short, strong fingers into the pot as he stirred with his free hand. Three, maybe four handfuls would trickle in, the pot rotating slightly on its axis as he stirred. It was never an attractive dish to us children but when my father prepared it on a Sunday morning, we consumed it without comment.

And sometimes for himself my father would prepare brose. It was a great source of energy to the farmers of the Muirton, he would tell us, though he never pushed it too heavily upon his children. He would dip his hand this time into a sack of oatmeal, place it in one of my mother's baking bowls and pour boiling water on it as he stirred it into a sticky, aesthetically offensive mass, and then eat it with a spoon directly from the bowl. It was a performance my mother would have considered "coarse," though she would never have expressed her opinion aloud. It seemed to be something a farmer with dirty hands would do in a humble cottage in a land far away—or something my father might expect a rough Canadian to do. He never appeared to be very keen on this terrible concoction. Perhaps his occasional brose mornings represented a rare trace of sentiment, of nostalgia, of past memories of the Muirton.

My father's most regular culinary creation on a Sunday morning was pancakes and syrup which, in itself, is a delightful dish; but my father was an innovator of the worst order. If he prepared the pancakes according to the standard recipe, they were perfectly acceptable, but he always thought he could improve upon them. He suffered from an impulse to drop various and sundry items into his batter, such as raisins or chopped walnuts or sometimes cornflakes or bran. The innovation that was most offensive to me, however, was the addition of bacon to the Sunday morning pancakes. Having once accepted one's pancakes, one had to eat them. To leave anything on one's plate was not only an open invitation to offend my father but it was also, because it was wasteful, a deadly sin. After having once tasted the dreadful mixture of bacon chips and pancakes, I thereafter accepted only the smallest single pancake; if by chance it was unblemished by his latest innovation, I could request a second helping.

The next ordeal was Sunday School. Maybe it was not quite an ordeal. It could be tolerated. At least there were a lot of other kids who had to go. It was not merely that we did not learn anything—what child, after all, actually thirsts for knowledge—but it prevented us from pursuing much more enjoyable pastimes such as building forts in trees or hunting squirrels with our slingshots in the bush down Burgess Street. But there was never any question but that we would attend Sunday School and church. My father would drive us a mile to the church where, led by him, we would sing old Moody hymns and be taught lessons in separate classes, after which my father would drive us all home to pick up my mother and return again to the regular morning service at 11:00 A.M. Usually one of us was allowed to stay home to keep the fire burning in the kitchen stove, to place potatoes on to boil at an hour prescribed by my mother, to see that the leek soup did not boil over and to baste the roast, which was either beef, pork or mutton in weekly rotation. Perhaps it was a Scottish custom to have one's heaviest meal on Sunday at 1:00 P.M. or so—after all, everything else we did was governed by our Scottish ancestry. But, alas, it was invariably my sister who was allowed to stay home to supervise the slow maturity of our Sunday dinner, probably, I imagine, because she was older and a girl.

As I said, I could tolerate Sunday School, but the hour and a half spent sitting restlessly in that great plain, barnlike church, with its hard, bare benches, its sober congregation and its dreary sermons, was the most trying part of my week. My mother usually sat with us, though she had a fine contralto voice and occasionally sat up in the choir when she sang a solo. My father regularly sat with the tenors. After the second hymn and second reading, the minister would pause, shuffle his papers on the pulpit, glance down condescendingly upon the young offspring—his captive audience—sitting obediently beside their parents, and begin a children's story. This was certainly my most uncomfortable moment. I would rather have been bored by the adult sermon, as every adult expected me to be. Could they possibly believe that a children's story would assuage my boredom with the adult sermon? I felt the minister was being patronizing to the citizens of tomorrow and that the adult congregation to a man was staring at me, expecting me to lean forward eagerly in my seat, and I had absolutely no inclination to do so. The children's stories had a moral to them and they were dull.

The rest of the time I just dreamed or I would watch Mr. Myers surreptitiously slip a candy into his mouth or maybe I would watch my father sitting beside Murdoch Mathieson and Mr. Moody over with the tenors. He sat in a plain old chair far out by the windows. He always seemed bored by the proceedings, though perhaps that was mere projection on my part. He would sketch in his hymn book or gaze dreamily out of the window at the summer sun filtering through the maple leaves; then at 11:30 or so the sermon would begin. At about the same

time a faint trace of interest would appear on his face as Mr.
Porter, who ran the street grader for the municipality, came
out to feed his chickens, just beyond the southern windows of
the church. There was a tremendous clucking and chattering of
hens, much, I am sure, to the minister's annoyance. But my
father's face would sharpen and his eyes seemed to lose their
dull glow with the clatter and clucking and flapping of wings.
Perhaps he went to church for our benefit.

It was the same during the Communion Service, which
occurred four times annually. Following the sermon, Flo
McCulloch—who was extremely active in the church, though
she never formally joined it—would slip quietly out the back
door of the choir, the congregation would drone, "Here, O my
Lord, I see thee face to face; here would I touch and handle
things unseen . . ." and my father, somewhat reluctantly it
seemed, would join the other elders at the communion table.
There were perhaps eight of them sitting behind that battered
old brown-painted table—though it was replaced in the 1930s
with a fine varnished hardwood one donated by the Douglas
family, in memory of their father, the minister who christened
me in that very church. The elders would serve the bread and
wine to the congregation, then to the minister, who then
served them. During this long period of relative inaction and
complete silence, except for the rattling of glasses in Mr.
Loban's palsied hands, my father would sit with his knees
crossed and his face in his hand, apparently in magnificent
disinterest. For years I thought it very strange that my father
would throw his head back and swallow that wine, for he
never touched alcoholic beverages. Mr. Philps, however, later
disillusioned me by pointing out that it was nothing but
Welch's Grape Juice purchased in Danny MacDonald's Gro-
cery Store. And I suppose the bread came from Shelley's Bakery
down on Tenth Street. This knowledge destroyed the mystery
of the ceremony for me. Forever after, when they sang, ". . .
here would I touch and handle things unseen . . ." I pictured

Danny MacDonald, dressed in his long white apron and bow tie, his hair parted down the middle, pushing a bottle of Welch's Grape Juice across the counter to Mr. Philps, or Mrs. Philps cutting up a loaf of Shelley's bread in her kitchen.

At any rate, my father always looked bored during the ceremony. Perhaps I am wrong in suggesting this, but whether it was boredom or not, those were moments when I had a certain empathy with my father. Certainly he became as animated as ever when it was all over and we would shuffle slowly out to the less inhibiting Sabbath afternoon, shaking hands soberly with the minister and much less soberly with Mrs. Taylor of the Ladies' Aid, who always had a little Scottish witticism to whisper in our ears.

That was church. My father must have paid some attention to the service, for if my mother made a comment on the sermon, my father would invariably answer, somewhat testily, "Och! He spoke a lot of gitter!" Which is another word I do not know how to spell, though there is no doubt that it is a form of Scottish baloney. I do not believe, however, that the church was an essential element in the maintenance of my father's moral standards. It was a firm foundation for his children, a foundation formed for him by his mother and his uncles in the North Church in Perth, and by their mothers and fathers before them. He no longer needed it for himself. The fact that a swear word was never uttered in his home, nor an ounce of liquor imbibed there, seemed to have nothing to do with the Gordon Presbyterian Church. It was something from far away—from the distant tramp of Prince Charles's feet on the North Inch, from the tenants of Gallowmuir and Muirton, from his own home, his own mother. It was, perhaps, inherited.

On Sunday afternoon my father allowed himself the liberty of removing his blue serge jacket, but he remained for the rest of the Sabbath dressed in his waistcoat, stiff white collar and tie. He read or drowsed peacefully in the living room or occasionally went for a walk or a drive with his family. We had a croquet lawn and a fine grass tennis court. It was a hive of activity six days a week with adults playing tennis or children playing soccer or baseball on it, but no one would even consider breaking the Sabbath.

In retrospect, my father's lassitude on Sundays was a most remarkable phenomenon, since he was perhaps the most energetic, industrious and enthusiastic person I have ever known. To while away the Sabbath afternoon in inactivity while his garden, his woodwork or his plans for the Fraser River remained untouched must have required considerable self-restraint, though it did not appear to take any effort on his part. This, too, was his inheritance from a far-off land, from generations of austere, puritanical Scottish tenant farmers. I did not consider my father God-fearing, at least in the sense that he did not spout religion and morals. The observance of the Sabbath, to keep it holy, was a legacy of the past, of Gallowmuir and the dusty road from Perth.

So also was his endless patience. If my infant eyes beheld my father's forested land in its virginity, my infant mind did not record the event. A more spectacular scene, however, was recorded slightly later and remains today. King and Skipper were two massive brown Clydesdales with great rounded rumps and noble heads, owned by Mr. MacMurray, a quiet, soft-spoken gentleman with refined features who lived up by the church. He did the rough landscaping on the Burgess Street side of our house. The portion nearest the street, where we later played croquet, was left at its natural slope, but one end of the potential tennis court, nearer the house, had to be dug out of the slope. Mr. MacMurray would wrestle with the two wooden handles of the great metal scoop, holding on to both reins in one hand as King and Skipper strained at the traces, their mighty chests heaving, their stocky legs leaning, the muscles of their great rumps rippling, and when the scoop was filled he would let it slide down to the lower end of the slope near Fourteenth, leaving a shining surface of black, damp earth behind him. Then he would heave up on the handles, the cutting edge of the scoop would dig into the earth and tip over, the handles almost striking the two huge Clydesdales. King and Skipper would amble easily back to scoop another load—and my father's tennis court slowly took shape.

My father preferred to do things with his own two hands, partly because he was an independent soul but mostly because he knew his were the only hands that could satisfy his craving for perfection. Yet the Clydesdales were necessary to tame the wild land, and my father, I am sure, loved those great beasts, so familiar to him on the distant Muirton. The rough work was done by the horses. My father did the rest with his pick and shovel and rake, with the sweat of his brow, and with his patience. And when it was finished, it was perfectly level, neat banks sloping upward at one end and downward at the other.

This perfection was not attained merely by chance or by rough visual reckoning. Although, again, I did not record it in my infant mind, there is nothing more certain than that my father set up his surveyor's transit, plunged its tripod legs into the soil, adjusted it till it was level, set his stakes, calculated his figures and presented King, Skipper and Mr. MacMurray with the exact information to level the land perfectly. There were no halfway measures with my father. You did the job perfectly from the beginning and it would remain perfect till the end of time.

On this huge expanse my father sowed seed and watched the grass appear. At first, if you stood erect, you could not see a blade of grass, but if you put your eye near the ground and looked down towards Fourteenth, you could see the first beautiful fresh green flush of new grass. My father watched it grow and he weeded it and cut it gently with his old hand mower. Then, next to the croquet lawn on the Burgess Street side, he planted shrubs and fruit trees which he purchased from yet another Scot, Mr. Livingstone, who had a nursery near Central

Park, and by the time he was finished, the area east of the driveway, which bisected his land, had grown into bush. My father cleared it with his own two hands. I saw him do it. I saw him squatting on his knees in the dusk, cutting and slashing and hacking, perspiration pouring down his face and soaking his shirt, enveloped in a great cloud of mosquitoes. There were splashes of blood on his bare forearms where he had killed his winged tormentors. He looked up and smiled at my mother and me that summer evening and my child's mind registered the beauty of that scene forever. As he wiped his face with the shirt of his upper arm, my mother told him he should stop; he had done enough for one day. My mother often told him that—and I never understood her concern. My father always worked that way; there was no other way to work.

In the area east of the driveway he cultivated a huge vegetable garden in the upper portion, added a wading pool and an hexagonal summerhouse surrounded by a boxwood hedge in the middle portion, and in the lower portion he laid a series of flower plots of various shapes. These were separated by winding cement walks, the pavement for which, with back-breaking labour and endless patience, he mixed and spread on Saturday afternoons and every evening until dark, unless he was interrupted by a manager's meeting, choir practice, Mr. Webster's weekly visit or the Sabbath.

But his labours had hardly begun. Before the vegetable garden was completely cleared, he spent days and weeks and months splitting the huge granite stones gathered from the land by Mr. MacMurray's Clydesdales. He would hold a drill in one hand, a heavy hammer in the other and pound and twist, pound and twist, pound and twist until he had drilled a two-inch-deep hole. He would bore a series of these in a line over the rock, then insert in each a pair of bent pieces of metal and a wedge—plug and feathers, he called them—and he would tap gently on each in rotation until there was a crack and a grind, and the great granite rock would open to show two beautiful, white and grey shining virgin surfaces. Some of these he used to form the rockery around the house. You can still see my father's drill holes in them. Others he cut into remarkably square blocks which he used to build the two pillars at the foot of the driveway. They were three feet square and six feet high. He was forced to purchase the cement from Gilley Brothers in New Westminster, but he refused to purchase sand—not, at least, when there was a gravel pit at the corner of Edmonds and Sixth Street. He threw a few old potato sacks into the McLaughlin Buick, drove up to the pit and, as I watched, filled them with sand.

The pillars rose slowly, kept perfectly vertical with the aid of my father's small, pointed brass plumb bob. He was a great plumb bob man, my father. You could find them in a number of nooks and crannies in our basement or in various drawers in the kitchen or dining room and sometimes even on his bedside table. He would use them for anything that had to be vertical— fence posts, gate posts, cement walls, the walls of the summer- house, table legs, and of course he used a plumb bob on the old one-inch water pipe that he placed precisely at the centre of each pillar. They were joined together by another pipe running under the roadway and were to act as a conduit for electrical wiring at some future date. And when the pillars at the foot of the driveway reached their prescribed height, my father cov- ered the top of each with a great slab of concrete which he made in a form and raised himself with the aid of an inclined plane. The hole he had made in the slab fitted perfectly over the central pipe.

The pillars remained like that for several years, during which they were wonderful for children to play upon. You could blow down the pipe on one pillar and push rain water up the other, preferably when Corkie or my little brother were preparing to blow down the other pipe. You could shoot rusty water right up in the air or two kids could blow at the same time, one on each end of the pipe, and whoever could not hold his breath any longer got a mouthful or a faceful of rusty water. But then my father spoiled our fun by placing wrought-iron stands over those pipes. That was one thing my father did not do himself, though I do not doubt for a moment that he could have, had he chosen to do so. He had old Alex McIntyre, the blacksmith on the government wharf, bend the metal for him. But my father cut and formed the lanterns from copper sheeting and he even cut the four glass windows for each of the lanterns, which were then screwed to the tops of the pipes. He never did connect up the electricity, but the pillars at the foot of the driveway stood there bravely at the entrance to my father's garden.

Perhaps it was before the pillars that he built the fences. The most intricate was a rustic fence along the Fourteenth Avenue front. In the old McLaughlin Buick we drove four or five miles to the woodland near Cariboo Road and there my father cut a batch of tall, thin second-growth cedars. It was, I suppose, public land, but it did not really matter; there was so much bush and forest around, no one really cared. The cedar poles were far too long and heavy to carry on the car, so my father tied them together in a bundle and towed them back home, dragging on the road across Second Street, Sixth Street and Douglas Road, like a tugboat towing a log boom.

Each section of the fence was a rectangle, the upper two-thirds crossed by half-lapped poles, the lower third filled in solidly with smaller vertical sticks of cedar. He did it all with his handsaw, his chisel, his hammer and the sweat of his brow. Patiently sawing, chipping, hammering—week after week, month after month, with occasional return trips to Cariboo Road for more cedar poles. He built a less intricate fence up Burgess Street and along the back and down the Douglas Road side. Patience, patience. Saw and chip and hammer, pound and twist, mix and spread.

In the long winter evenings he was no less active. Each year he had a special project planned for his workshop: a standard lamp, a chest of drawers, a lady's bureau, a desk—upon which I now write—and a magnificent bed, the head and foot of which he cut from the huge hardwood steering wheel of one of the older Fraser River stern-wheelers, *Samson*. It was six feet in diameter inside the spokes; he found it stored away in a shed and carried it home on the top of our 1929 Nash. He designed each piece of furniture himself and carefully drew the plans to scale on dimpled white draughting paper. He would use only hardwood, held together with dowels and glue. Nails he considered an abomination and varnish most distasteful. Every piece of furniture was French-polished with figure-eight strokes. Coat after coat. Patience, endless patience—and satisfaction.

Another project so typical of my father was the manufacture of a croquet set. He had purchased a set from Mac and Mac's in New Westminster, but almost immediately he recognized it as a pitiful example of North American ineptitude. Within a week, the mallet heads shattered and the balls split. The smallest child could bend the flimsy hoops. My father drew his plans and searched the docks and lumber yards for material he knew would last forever. The handles he made from sturdy maple poles which he patiently planed into hexagonal shapes. The mallet heads he made from several hardwoods—oak and maple and lignum vitae. They, too, were hexagonal with grooves cut towards each end, painted in a colour to correspond with the balls. He left them in their natural grain and French-polished each except for the maple ones, which were designed for children and were lighter. They were magnificent mallets, far more durable, far more beautiful than you could buy in a store. But my father knew his limitations. He imported the croquet balls from Joe Anderson's, a shop we knew well even though it was five thousand miles away in Perth. Red, blue, yellow and black. In their many years of use, not one fleck of paint was chipped from them. The hoops he had made to his design by a blacksmith. No child would ever consider trying to bend them.

Then, at some point in the winter, he would receive a seed catalogue from Dobbie's in Edinburgh. He would prowl through this volume by the hour, making notes, and finally he would send off his order. Before the seeds arrived, he would sketch the outlines of his garden in a little loose-leaf book and list every variety of plant and the number to be placed in each plot in his garden. When the great box of seeds arrived from Edinburgh, every warm, sunny corner of the house was crammed with seed flats. A load of manure would appear and my father would start his long, laborious task of digging the vegetable garden—one spadeful deep, the brown earth tipped upside down on the previous row and prodded to loosen its winter consistency. And in every second trough he would lay a solid line of thick, wet cow manure. Occasionally he would stop to wipe the sweat from his brow or to throw a worm to the robins who always seemed to know when my father was digging in his garden. He would watch for a moment, amused, then slide his spade down again until his foot touched the damp spring earth. No one could work more diligently than my father, but some vague echo from the past always reminded him of the Sabbath, to keep it holy.

There were numerous tasks my father performed about the house or in the garden. If he broke the handle of his hoe or rake, he would make a new one himself. He said he could make a better job of anything he could buy in Mac and Mac's or Trapp's. He made his own grass edger. When he needed metal letters for the name of his house, he found an old sheet of aluminum and laboriously cut out the letters for Gannochy (a contraction of his family home, Gannochyfold) and screwed them into the huge gates he had swung from the pillars at the foot of the driveway. He made a set of fireboxes for the fireplace from sheets of copper, pressing out his favourite emblem on them, the Scottish thistle. He built our first radio, a crystal set with earphones. He repaired broken clocks, developed his own photographs, soled his own garden boots; and once he won a prize in a crossword puzzle contest for printing the solution—with the aid of a magnifying glass—on the back of a postage stamp.

There was hardly anything my father could not do, a fact that was accepted quite indifferently by his family. Indeed it was Lars who really brought the beauty of our home to my attention. In the first year of World War II I found a summer job in Mercer's shipyard on the Fraser. One day I was helping Lars with some work on a naval seiner. "You live quite near us, Lars," I said to him. The old Scandinavian finished hammering in a nail, spat a great blob of tobacco juice onto the scaffolding and asked, "Where the hell do you live?" When I told him at the corner of Fourteenth and Burgess, Lars thought for a moment and then remarked, "You're crazy like hell. A goddamned prince lives there."

The tenant farmers of the Muirton were hardly peasants, but certainly they were not princes of any adjectival genus. My father was a civil engineer, though I had no idea how he became one. We accepted the old post office building in New Westminster at the corner of Sixth and Columbia as our father's place of work and we often visited him there, in the casual manner of the day. Just inside the Sixth Street door of the building, an old gentleman would pull a lever and his caged elevator would carry us slowly but smoothly up to the third floor where we would see a great high door, its sweeping brown grain varnished in its natural state and, on a panel near the bottom, in plain black letters, the awesome words, "Dominion Public Works Department." It was a beautiful door, and the hall into which it led was even higher, and always dark and cool and quiet, but you could smell the office there in that cool, dark hallway. Odours? Of what? Draughting paper? India ink? Old leather in which the engineer's instruments were always encased? I do not know what the odours were but they were distinctive to that office. In the draughting room there were high stools with worn rungs and sloping tables covered with all the paraphernalia of the engineer: heavy, white, dimpled draughting paper or grey-blue linen tracing paper—which would magically turn into pure white linen cloth if you washed it in hot water; celluloid set squares and T squares and beautiful bone rulers delicately etched; pens holding nibs of all sizes and shapes; India ink in conical bottles and, beside them, a little square of cloth to wipe the pen nib clean; compasses and protractors and heavy metal parallel rulers on little grooved rollers which rumbled as we rolled them up and down our father's draughting table; and strangely shaped celluloid cut into sweeping curves or sharp curves, to fit any line an engineer could possibly wish to draw.

It was an awesome and solemn event to walk uncertainly into that huge, silent draughting room where Mr. Cunningham, Mr. Cox, Jack Saint and my father toiled on their high wooden stools. They would stop their work, rotate upon their seats and twist their feet through the worn rungs of their stools. Jack Saint would smile broadly, blink his eyes nervously and offer some sly witticism to make us laugh. On a rare occasion, my father would lead us into the next room to meet the two stenographers, Isa MacDonald and Cora Passmore. It was a neater room, a more female room, a less friendly room—but our visit there was only a momentary one, perhaps because the door to the next room was labelled in bold, black letters, C. C. Worsfold, respectfully referred to in the draughting room as "the boss." His was the inner sanctum, into which small feet never strayed. Although his was a household name, I do not ever recall seeing him, and it was not until many years later that I saw the office itself, with my father sitting behind the great oaken desk.

The draughting room was a pleasant place with its musty odours, mysterious instruments and my father's friends, but this was just a portion of his professional life. He would occasionally take my brother and me to the clay dykes near the mouth of the river where he would survey a small area for an hour or so. Perhaps this was merely an excuse to allow us to pick blackberries which grew in great profusion along the dykes, or to fish from one of his secret bars. He would set up his transit and peer through it with the brim of his felt hat bent upward and backward over his forehead, allowing him to snuggle in closely to his lens. In those days, a surveyor could always be instantly recognized by the proud upward sweep of his hat brim above a tanned, weatherbeaten face.

Occasionally my father would take us to a spot on the river where the mud-streaked tender *Pelly* picked us up and carried us to one of the dredges—the *Mastodon,* the *Fruhling* or the *King Edward.* They were clumsy, muddy, immobile beasts; the *Mastodon* disgorged muddy water from its endless chain of buckets into the maws of waiting barges, while the others sucked silt and gravel through a long line of pipes, spewing out the contents on the distant shore.

The dredges were hardly exciting, but the *Samson*—the *Samson* was different. It was a fine old stern-wheeler built on a scowlike hull, with a towering A frame on the foredeck for pulling out snags or replacing lights or bells or spar-buoys in the river channel. There were many wonders to be seen on the *Samson,* but perhaps the greatest was to stand at the stern on the middle deck and watch the red blades of the stern-wheel slash into the grey waters of the Fraser, to emerge a moment later streaming with water—up and over and down again, spinning and slashing and dripping. You could never tire of watching it. Or the engine room where Frank Creeden kept everything spotless. You could run your hand down the length of the cream-painted boilers and your hand would come away as clean as it went on— and sometimes cleaner. And down there you could watch the two huge arms of the pistons driving the great red stern-wheel—back and up and down, back and up and down—and if you stood at the right angle you could see past the arms and through the port to the wheel itself, spinning and slashing and dripping.

The *Samson* was easily the most fascinating part of my father's work. You could climb up into the wheelhouse and stand beside Tommy Hurst, the mate, who always wore an old felt hat, or beside Captain Jimmy Rogers. A huge man he was, with a very red face peering out severely from beneath his white peaked cap, like a veritable Admiral of the Blue. Sometimes they would let you hold the wheel—and once old Captain Rogers picked me up with one hairy hand around my waist, placed my hand on the cord that blew the steam whistle, put his other hairy paw over mine, and pulled downward. The cord cut into my hand so deeply that I did not hear the *Samson*'s hoarse, deep wheeze—but the Westminster Bridge opened for us as I rubbed the deep crease from my hand.

It was a momentary incident—perhaps I did not later even mention it to my mother—but it was one that would forever remain with me: the pain of the whistle cord in my hand, the fear of the awesome captain picking me up with one large hairy paw. At the time I did not know that Captain James Rogers was the nephew of Jerry Rogers, the mighty spar man who logged the shores of Burrard Inlet for Captain Edward Stamp's sawmill in the earliest days of the inlet. I did not know that the young Jimmy Rogers and his family had helped to evacuate the youthful City of Vancouver when it burned to the ground in 1886, before the railway arrived.

My father would have been only slightly interested, had he known. He lived in the present—and the present on those soft summer days on the river was his work in the wheelhouse of the *Samson* with Captain Rogers and Tommy Hurst. He was always up there in the wheelhouse. He would pull the leather strap fastened to the base of the window and ease it down carefully into its slot. He would lean out far above the foredeck and watch the *Samson* slide slowly up to a snag. He would watch the deck hands slip a chain over the half-sunken log, the steam winch would hiss and smoke and the mighty A frame would drag the snag onto the deck. When four or five of these logs had been collected, Captain Rogers would head for the shore and run the square nose of his ship right up on the bank, the winch would hiss and roar, the chain would tighten, and the snags would spin through the air to land in a tangled mass far up on the bank of the river. Captain Rogers would shout down the polished brass speaking tube to Frank Creeden in the engine room, the great red stern-wheel would reverse and the *Samson* would back off into the river.

My father watched intently as the snags were pulled and dumped, as the bulbous metal buoys and long spar-buoys were placed gently in the Fraser, exactly where he told the skipper to place them. He loved the activity on the river. It was a relaxing day for him, watching from the open window. But the job that seemed to tie his whole professional life together was the sounding. They must have had a line to follow, though I was not conscious of one. A man dressed in a rubber apron stood on the foredeck by the A frame and cast his weighted sounding line well ahead of the slowly moving *Samson,* and as the line became vertical, he would read the mark and turn to shout the number up to my father. His brown leather sounding book was spread in one hand, the stub of a pencil in the other, and with each shout my father would press the number deeply into the blue-lined page—indeed he pressed so hard you could read the number through two or three succeeding pages. Back and forth across the river, his face becoming more tanned as the summer progressed, his receding hair lifting gently in the river breeze, his face intent. The faint thrash of the great red wheel at the stern, the creak of Captain Rogers's wheel and the bark of the lineman down on the foredeck. And my father at work.

Perhaps it was these strange numbers that my father transposed to his grey-blue linen tracing paper on those less exciting days in the draughting room—transposed into clear, black lines with his celluloid set squares and T squares, his bone rulers and his India ink, into neat numbers and letters which bore my father's personal imprint. Rock fills and dykes and channels and buoys.

The Fraser was my father's consuming interest, as far as his professional life was concerned. During our evening meals he would discuss the depth of the North Arm, the length of the south jetty or the stupidity of what he always referred to only as "Ottawa." The capital city of the Dominion had distinctly unpleasant connotations in our home. It fell into the same class of words as "Englishman" or "Canadian," though there was no racial inference. "Ottawa" was merely the word my father chose to represent eastern apathy and ignorance of the west. The rest of us ate our evening meal silently with our own thoughts, only my mother endeavouring valiantly to show some interest in the subject. As he was dealing a hand of cribbage to Mr. Webster on a Friday evening, he would ramble on continuously over the lack of interest of the government in the east. "Ottawa has no mortal conception of what is going on out here," he would rage. "Fifteen two, fifteen four and six are ten. If the deputy minister would listen to Tom Reid . . ." And so it would go.

You can perhaps understand, then, the crisis in our home when my father was told, some time in the early thirties, that he would have to move to Ottawa for at least a year if he expected any advancement in the civil service. It was the first time I can recall my father being deeply depressed and worried. How could he leave his garden, his home, the church and the river? How could he uproot his whole family and move to the east? The strain and uncertainty went on for weeks—but a decision was finally made. I can remember my father walking across the tennis lawn one late summer afternoon to where my mother and I were sitting beneath the apple tree. His face was lined with worry. He said he had refused to go, even though it meant there would be no more promotions. It was magnificent news to his family, though it meant the end of my father's professional ambitions.

It is impossible to judge which was my father's greatest interest—the river, his garden, his woodworking or the church. He put every ounce of his energy into each in turn, yet he still found time for his family. When we were small, he told us stories as we stretched out on our beds in our pyjamas. There were magnificent tales, at least for boys, of guddling for trout with Tommy Lawrie on the Esperson Farm (where it was we did not know) or hunting for rabbits with Jimmy Lawrie or placing a ferret at one end of a rabbit warren and catching the poor beast as it raced out the other. On one occasion, my father told us, he reached for the ferret's head to recapture it as it hesitated at the burrow exit, but it turned its head and sank its canine teeth through his thumb—and he demonstrated this to us dramatically by clasping his injured thumb between the index finger and the thumb of his other hand. There was his vivid tale of lifting the haystacks in the autumn at the Muirton. There was always a mound of chaff remaining at the centre of the lifted stack, he said, and it would move gently as if there were some living creature beneath it. When the farm dogs saw this, they raced in to grasp the rats which had sheltered and fed there, and flung them over their shoulders, only to grasp another and another till by the end of the day they were covered with blood. Any rats that escaped the dogs were clubbed to death by my father and his brother. His stories describing the manufacture of laminated plywood or of paper were much less interesting.

My father also shared his interest in sports with us. We knew that he had played rugby in his youth since in our attic there was a remarkably small velvet cap with a tarnished silver tassel attached to its crown upon which was engraved, again in tarnished silver, the coat of arms of his county, Perthshire, and the dates on which he had won this prize. He bought us several rugby balls over the years and often in the evening he would suspend his evening garden chores to stand at the far end of the tennis court and drop-kick the ball to a group of neighbourhood children standing down at the Fourteenth Avenue end. Frequently the ball would sail over our heads and out onto the street. In the summer he would play tennis with us, and at least

once each fall he would drive us to Steveston to bar fish. He
would build a fire for us and we would huddle around it
eating sandwiches salted with sand and streaked with salmon
eggs, and when we got home we would have to stand on the
furnace grate to thaw our frozen limbs. On the Twenty-fourth
of May—a much more important day in our province than
Dominion Day—he would bundle us all into the Nash and take
us to a picture show in Vancouver and then to dinner at
Purdy's.

Rugby and cricket were my father's sports in his youth, and
quite often he would drive those of us who wished to go to
Brockton Point to watch the All-Blacks or the Maoris, visiting
from New Zealand, play a local side, but at some point he
developed an interest in North American sports. In the late
twenties and early thirties he would take us to New Westminster to watch Max Shiles, Bill Gifford, Jack D'Easum and Hop
Wilkie play basketball, and prior to the war when box lacrosse
became popular, my father and his children were regular
attenders. Occasionally he would drive us to Vancouver to see
Guy Patrick's Lions play ice hockey, a sport familiar only to
those British Columbians who listened to the games over the
radio on Saturday evenings.

Perhaps my father's interest in North American sports events
was the first sign that he was changing—indeed, his children
were becoming old enough to affect his tastes. This became
more apparent at some point prior to the war when he began
to put on his old clothes after our noon Sunday dinner and
would spend the remainder of the afternoon weeding his
flower plots. On that first occasion, it must have been an
historical and perhaps fearful moment for him. Centuries of
pious Sabbaths came to an end. There was a Sunday, too, when
my sister and a friend calmly tightened the tennis net and
proceeded to play for the remainder of the afternoon. I waited
for my father to come storming out, but he did not, and
neither my sister nor her friend were struck lifeless by a bolt

from heaven. Somehow, too, the old objections to Englishmen and Canadians were diminished, though not completely abandoned.

But little else changed at that time. There was still no swearing, no alcohol in our home, and his sons' daily and weekly tasks still had to be completed strictly on time. Our duties were to fill the wood box for the kitchen stove, thin the carrots and lettuce in the vegetable garden, weed the flower plots and cut the huge expanse of lawn every Saturday, whether it needed it or not. We had our family duties, and failure to complete them would bring the wrath of my father down upon us.

Our mother would always intercede on our behalf at such times, much to our father's annoyance. We were much closer to her. Other than my father's gifts of baseballs and rugby balls and our frequent attendance at basketball or lacrosse games, there was little outward sign of affection between us. Perhaps it was Scottish reserve, but it applied also to relations between my mother and father. We were hardly a kissing family. On their wedding anniversary—fourth of July—our parents always drove to Vancouver for dinner and a movie, while, in the early days at least, Flo McCulloch or Mrs. Gibson baby-sat in our house. The next morning we would find beside our beds a small box or jar of barley sugar or Edinburgh Rock, purchased in the little candy shop beside the Orpheum Theatre. But these were my mother's gifts—at least I always considered them so. She was a more affectionate parent, softening the criticism my father often directed at his children, who did not appreciate the boundless energy he expended on his work at home or in his profession. Nor did we appreciate his kindness.

I had greater empathy with my mother. She and her family were more sensitive individuals. The Murdochs were carriers and coach trimmers in the Moray villages of Elgin and Forres not far from Culloden, unfamiliar with the musket and broadsword of the unruly clans to the north and west. They lived there until my maternal grandfather, a tailor and cutter, married a bootmaker's daughter and settled in a house named Dunearn on Balhousie Street in Perth, just a few steps from the southern border of the Muirton Farm.

They raised a family of three daughters and two sons, each of whom was more artistically inclined than my father. They sang in church choirs, in public concerts, in operettas, and acted on the local stage. One daughter, my Auntie Elsie, became a regular contributor to a strange little monthly paper named *The People's Friend*—or more affectionately, *The Peeps*—and she later published a novel in which relatives in Canada played a minor role. They were a close-knit family. When my mother heard Handel's *Messiah* at Christmas or Easter, she would become nostalgic and dreamy-eyed, and sadly tell us that she could still hear her father's tenor voice echoing through the halls of Dunearn as he sang "Comfort ye, comfort ye, my people, saith your God" and "Every valley shall be exalted, and every mountain and hill made low; the crooked straight, and the rough places plain."

The Murdochs were a gentler race. They did not have the energy, the intensity, the enthusiasm of my father. They would never have considered emigrating to Canada. They would never have sweated amidst a cloud of mosquitoes to clear the land on Fourteenth Avenue; they would never have stood, keen and interested, at Captain Rogers's wheelhouse window as the lead man called up his numbers from the foredeck; they would never have constructed, from the wheel of the *Samson*, my father's magnificent bed. And they would never have, slowly and patiently, raised the pillars at the foot of the driveway.

two

As I have said, most of our family friends were immigrants from various towns and villages in Scotland, and to every family name we could add its village of origin. The McCullochs, for instance, were from Oban, which perhaps helped in our understanding of them. For better or for worse, their family was more closely intertwined with ours than with any other. I do not know why this was so, for they had no children to tie the families together and certainly they were a proud, haughty lot. Perhaps it was my mother's kind, sympathetic disposition which allowed ours to be one of the few families to accept them, or perhaps they were my father's earliest friends. Certainly they arrived before my father. Flo McCulloch once told me that they lived on Kingsway when it was still called Westminster Avenue, which dates their arrival to some time around the turn of the century.

It is difficult to understand why they left such a beautiful, quiet corner of the globe. Oban was—and still is—a lovely little fishing village tucked away in a fold of the Western Highlands across the Firth of Lorne from the Island of Mull and all the other fascinating islands of the Inner Hebrides: Staffa and Iona, Colonsay, Islay, Jura, and so many others. Perhaps it was for economic reasons, though even this is difficult to accept, since they lived in a magnificent home on Kingsway, half a block from the end of Fourteenth Avenue. Furthermore, there was never a mention of a Mr. McCulloch, suggesting that they must have had some financial security before they left the Western Highlands, and no one to my knowledge was ever unwise enough to ask such a personal question of the proud Highlanders at the end of the street.

They were certainly there before my father and before my mother and therefore before me and they blend easily into that blurred panorama of early images—of the McLaughlin Buick and Mr. MacMurray's massive Clydesdales and my father splitting the granite rocks for the pillars at the foot of the driveway. At that time Mrs. McCulloch was still alive, though her name to us children was completely unpronounceable. McCulloch originally emerged from my sister's childish lips as Mi-cah, and Mi-cah she was for the rest of her days. It was not until long after her death that I realized this was not her proper name, that it was not just another strange West Highland name.

Mi-cah was a frail, elderly little woman, her fine grey hair neatly parted down the centre of her small, delicate head and swept back into a small bun. The skin of her face was thin and delicate, almost transparent, with a glow of pinkness in her cheeks and fine little wrinkles that somehow made her the picture of simplicity, sweetness and kindness. She spoke little, perhaps because her native tongue was Gaelic, though she understood everything that was said. Her eyes would glow and sparkle and she would nod assent, and a pretty little smile would shine across her delicate features. But Mi-cah had rheumatism. Her hands were grotesquely deformed and useless. The disease must also have been present in her legs, for she used to be able only to shuffle along cautiously and slowly, her small felt boots peeking out from below her long woollen skirt, until one day she tripped and broke her hip. She lived for the remainder of her days in a wheelchair or was carried about from one chair to another.

Her daughters, Flo and Isabel—or Belle, as her family called her—were about my parents' age, though they would never dream of divulging the dates of their births and certainly no one would dare to ask them. They could be considered, even in the earliest days, as being only reasonably slender—or perhaps relatively slender would be more correct, since in later years their bulk increased remarkably. From photographs taken as long ago as 1912, however, they were both rather attractive and quite slim. Flo, the younger, had an open type of prettiness, but there was no languid passion burning in her dark eyes as there was in her sister's. Isabel had a more oval face, finer features, a delicate white skin and dark hair thrown back almost carelessly. She would have been a beauty in any age, though she never married and never, as far as is known, had the opportunity of doing so. She was, after all, surrounded by Canadians, and it is difficult to imagine her finding a High-lander, far less a Lowlander, who was good enough for her. In addition, she was somewhat eccentric and extremely proud and reserved. Flo's and Isabel's figures were impossible to evaluate since their apparel did not permit such a judgement. There had also been a brother, Duncan, but he had died soon after World War I, leaving a wife, Nessie, who promptly returned to her homeland.

The other member of the household was a fellow named Emerson Doran who, quite surprisingly, was a Canadian—and about as Canadian as anyone could be, according to my father's standards which, in general, were the standards of the McCul-lochs. It will always be a mystery how Em ever found a foothold in that family except that there was never a more friendly, more kind, more good-humoured man. Perhaps he had been Duncan's friend. In the earliest days he lived in an old unfinished shed by the church but later became a boarder in that magnificent old house on Kingsway. He was part owner of and truck driver for the Edmonds Coal and Wood Yard, along with the MacMurrays of Clydesdale fame.

Em had an Irish face with a broad Irish grin, though he was originally from Ontario. Perhaps his dark complexion was the result of an Iberian ancestor or perhaps it was the result of his occupation as a coal handler. Certainly his hands were deeply pigmented with coal dust. He had a gravelly voice which always seemed about to burst into laughter. Em rarely spoke without a broad grin or an infectious, rasping laugh. He had a blue serge suit for his infrequent sallies to the Gordon Presbyterian Church, but usually when he was not in his grimy working clothes he wore a shirt and sweater or a tweed jacket. Only occasionally did Em wear a tie, an accessory considered quite un-Canadian, though perhaps its presence could be attributed to the good influence of the McCullochs and other upstanding members of the Scottish community.

Their home was of Victorian design with typical British Columbian modifications. The floor space must have been astronomical, though a good portion of this expanse was occupied by a broad verandah extending all along the front and halfway down the southern side, supported by a series of round wooden columns. This was covered by a shingle roof, sloping up to the second floor, on top of which was another roof broken into what seemed to be a hundred graceful gables, with smaller gables above them. One of the two large gables facing Kingsway covered a bedroom with a large bay window, and the other shaded a balcony, at the outer ends of which were two round columns connected below by an ornate balustrade decorated with a long flower box.

It was a magnificent house, from the wide, cool verandah to the roof of a hundred gables. At the front door there was a bell which you rang by twisting a handle. In my day it was so old and worn that it tinkled only weakly. Inside that door was a room which was always referred to as the hall, though it was almost as large as some of the houses in Burnaby. From it a great broad staircase wound upward to the bedrooms, painting rooms, sewing rooms, storerooms and intricate halls and passageways. At the back of the house, another set of stairs led down again to the kitchen. It was quite a large kitchen with a long, narrow scullery at one end, though there was hardly room to move in it: there was the usual coal and wood stove and tables and chairs but the rest of the room was cluttered with various items which we secretly referred to as junk—old dusty bottles and dishes, dried flowers, pieces of driftwood, mysterious boxes, and piles and piles of newspapers. Certainly everyone used a few pages of newspaper to light the stove in the morning, but there was no apparent need to store all the rest, particularly in the kitchen—except that it happened to be the *Vancouver Sun,* and the *Sun* Sunday funny papers were different from those of the *Province,* to which my father subscribed. Flo did not keep those newspapers for our use, though we had great fun digging out the Sunday funnies and reading them on the back stairs, since there was never any room to sit down in the kitchen.

It was a magnificent, cluttered, mysterious home, but the most magnificent part of all was the balcony. It was our custom to spend a Sunday afternoon at the McCullochs' early in July when the cherries were black with ripeness. My father would drive us down in the McLaughlin Buick. He would turn up Kingsway, pass the house and make a U turn at Stride Avenue so that he could park in the vacant lot beside the house. Once when he made that U turn, the back door of the car became unfastened and my sister went hurtling out onto Kingsway. She just got up, climbed back in and did not seem to have hurt herself at all. Of course she did not pick any cherries. She sat up on the balcony with the adults while my brother and I did the picking. Actually, we never stayed away very long, perhaps because we had the feeling that we had merely been got rid of by the adults or because we tired of picking or because we soon became sated with cherries; but certainly we always wanted to get up to the balcony where the adults and our sister sat.

Mi-cah was invariably just outside the door with a sweet smile on her face, silent, yet absorbing everything; and Isabel, dressed so stylishly and artistically, sitting with a small harp on her knee, picking out some languid Scottish air; and Flo overflowing the wooden chair she sat on; and Em lounging casually, talking, smiling and laughing with my mother and father. It was cool and quiet and high up there. You felt as if you were floating amongst the trees. If you stood on the lower rail of the balustrade and looked over the lobelia and geraniums in the flower box, you could see, far below, the weathered cement walk on which was printed—upside down from the balcony—the name of the McCullochs' house, Lorne Villa, surely suggesting that they had built the house and named it after the firth on which they had once lived. The cherry tree almost touched the balcony on one side, and on the other, rowan trees with great clusters of bright orange berries drooped pendulously right to the edge of the balcony where you could pick them and shoot them surreptitiously at your sister when no one was looking. Occasionally a streetcar or automobile would pass outside the row of rowan trees that grew along the iron fence and up to the gate—which clinked metallically as it was closed—but mostly there was silence except for the soft tones of Isabel's harp and the quiet mutter of conversation. It was a peaceful spot. Once, though, many years later when we were visiting the McCullochs at Christmas, I slipped up the winding staircase from the hall just to look out again from the balcony, but it was cold and the lobelias and geraniums were gone and the rowan trees were leafless and Mi-cah and Flo and Em and Isabel and the harp were not there, and I was much older—and I was sorry I had come.

The McCullochs' garden was another beautiful spot. It was not a perfectly groomed garden. The grass was not thick and soft and green and weedless. You did not stand and gaze upon it from afar; you sat or walked or played upon its informality. There were rowan and cherry trees at the front and side and at the back a grove of cedars, firs and hemlocks beside rough, shady paths and half-hidden rustic seats. All down the north side and swinging around to the back of the house, coarse grass, closely cut, rolled unevenly as if it had never been landscaped, as if it had never been sown by hand. Along the borders were lupines and daisies and primroses, interspersed occasionally with little artificial pools of water. And in the centre of the grass at the back was a large square of boards covering a well which echoed to the tramp of childish feet. There was an old wooden wheelbarrow back there too, filled with earth and planted with anemones or pansies or maybe gazanias. We played golf on that sloping, rolling grass—and on the Sabbath afternoon. It seemed to be accepted when you were visiting, provided you kept your tie and waistcoat on.

It was a wonderful home and the McCullochs were wonderful people, though Flo and Isabel were without a doubt the proudest, most stubborn and most sensitive people imaginable, to the point of paranoia. They used to walk up Fourteenth on a summer evening for a game of tennis, Isabel always dressed stylishly in a long white dress, a coloured bandana about her head. They invariably arrived too late for a complete set—tardiness was another of their characteristics—but they enjoyed themselves, as did the five or six children sitting about on the periphery, snickering at the old folk playing tennis. When it was all over one evening, however, a rude child said to Isabel, "You know, Isabel, Mrs. Gibson says you're too fat to play tennis." A look of indignant rage appeared on her fine features. "Oh! She does, does she! We'll see about that!" she snapped and immediately turned out the back gate with her racquet still in her hand—up Burgess Street, a bunch of kids dancing about her, up past Mrs. Crawford's house. It seemed unbelievable. Surely she would not do it. And the child suddenly became frightened as Isabel turned into Gibson's garden. "She really didn't say it, Isabel, she really didn't say it," he admitted. There, just a few yards from the unsuspecting Mrs. Gibson, Isabel stopped, hissed in disgust and swiped at the child with her tennis racquet. She stamped back to our place, and not another word was said about it.

Isabel, like the others, was proud of her ancestry, though at times it reached ridiculous heights. She once told us of a conversation at a meeting of the Imperial Order Daughters of the Empire, of which she was a member. A stranger, no doubt trying valiantly to melt Isabel's icy reserve, remarked to her, "You are Scottish, are you not, Miss McCulloch?" Even as she told the story, Isabel's fine features hardened. Her back straightened, she spun around to the imaginary stranger and she spat out the proud words, "I am not! I am Hieland!" and she walked haughtily away. This was too much even for my mother and father, who were perfectly satisfied with being merely Scottish. On another occasion one of us, perhaps bored with the dinner conversation, which ranged from Dundee to Perth to Oban, asked as innocently as possible, "Oban's in England, isn't it, Isabel?" She turned and snapped, "It is not!" Perhaps she realized that she was being teased, or perhaps she realized it was, after all, Christmas, for she said no more but turned away and resumed her conversation.

Isabel was certainly artistically inclined. If she had lived in the seventies or eighties she would probably have been recognized as a prominent local artist. In the twenties and thirties she was merely an eccentric with a strange hobby and a useless talent. From memory she would paint West Highland scenes in oil or, in the summer, she would find a rock in West Vancouver or on Bowen Island, sit on it by the hour and sketch the rugged coastline of her adopted home. Later she would complete the task in water colours. Or she would collect shells and cut miniature flowers from cloth to form framed mosaics. And on the walls of their great dining room she painted woodland scenes—tall, sweeping birches bending in the wind and long grass and wild flowers, or pools and ponds and mountains, or sailing ships and beacons on a rocky headland. You never knew what you were going to see on the walls of the McCullochs' great dining room when you visited there.

Em, as I have said, was the most good-humoured man I have ever known. He had to be; he succumbed to the Highland charms of Miss Flora McCulloch in 1928, the year before our McLaughlin Buick succumbed to the Nash. The wedding took place on a beautiful, warm Sunday afternoon—though perhaps it only seemed to be a Sunday afternoon since I had to dress in my Sunday clothes. The ceremony took place in the house on Kingsway. At the time, this did not seem strange to me, since weddings do not often play a very important part in a six-year-old's life. In retrospect, however, it was rather remarkable. Flo had been one of the most active workers in the Gordon Presbyterian Church since its inception, shortly before my father's arrival. She was a member of the choir, singing with the sopranos, occasionally as a soloist, in a sweet though untrained voice, and she was a member of that choir for the remainder of her days. Flo just did not change her habits easily. The other church activity to which she clung with remarkable fidelity was that of providing the flowers for the Sabbath service. Every Saturday night of the year she would walk or be driven by Em to the church with an armful of flowers obtained from various sources, but usually from her own garden. No one else ever performed this task—and only those few who attended the annual congregational meeting were aware of it. Every year at this gathering, the minister would faithfully express his appreciation of her weekly task and Flo, on the one occasion when I was present, sat there massively filling her chair, smiling and simpering in apparent embarrassment. She always said there was no need for Mr. MacCrae to thank her, though if he had not, Flo would have lashed at him unmercifully for at least three Tuesdays and Fridays at our kitchen table.

There was no greater certainty in my childhood world of the twenties and thirties than that Flora McCulloch would be at choir practice on Thursday evening, that she would place some floral offering in the church on Saturday evening and that she would be there amongst the sopranos on the Sabbath morning. But never in the fifty years of serving the church did she ever formally join it. She never confessed her faith; she never, as it were, signed on the dotted line. Perhaps it was because of her Highland pride and reticence—but of course no one would ever dare to ask her for fear of being slain verbally on the spot. Almost certainly her refusal did not stem from a disbelief in the Trinity or the Apostle's Creed. She probably believed implicitly in both. But she was damned—if you'll pardon the expression, dear Flo—she was damned if she would get down on her knees and admit it to the Reverend Peter MacCrae and all those blessed old elders who were not one whit better than she. At any rate, the fact that she never formally joined the church was the reason for her slipping out just before the celebration of communion and, I believe, for not having her wedding formalized in the church.

It was a great event. Six-year-old children, of course, were not allowed to get close enough to see the nuptials, though my sister did, since she was a flower girl. It was more fun after the ceremony in the garden, where people talked and ate and had their photographs taken. Flo wore a very plain fawn dress with a loop of small flowers embroidered around the front, a belt that encompassed her lower abdomen, cotton stockings and laced shoes. Em was resplendent in his freshly pressed blue serge suit, and Isabel wore a long white dress with a broad scarlet tie around the neck—and she carried a magnificent, multicoloured Japanese parasol. Mi-cah was there too, as sweet as could be, smiling and nodding in a long purple gown with flowered sleeves.

The marriage made no difference to anyone's life as far as I was concerned. Em had always been a bona fide member of the family anyway, and Flo continued her usual regularized life. I suppose she did her washing on Mondays like everyone else, though I could not honestly vouch for this, Mondays being far too busy a day for anyone to socialize. But on Tuesday afternoon, without fail, Flo's ever-increasing mass would come through our back gate, she would take those quick little steps along the cement walk, enter the back door and implant herself on the built-in bench behind our kitchen table. It was such a foolish place for her to sit, since there was very little space between the end of the table and the arm of the bench. She had probably sat there regularly in those happier days when she was slender, and Flo was not one to change her habits. Indeed, the predictability of her Tuesday visits was, at times, most trying for my mother, who sometimes had other things to do on that particular day. Flo, on the other hand, assumed that Tuesday was her day and my mother could plan her week accordingly. There was nothing in their unwritten contract that said my mother could do anything else but entertain Flo on Tuesday afternoons. If my mother summoned up the courage to explain that she had an unavoidable appointment elsewhere, there was a terrible scene. Flo's face would tighten and she would snap, "Oh! I suppose you're going to have Mrs. Stuart in instead!" or "Oh! I suppose you're going to Mrs. Healy's. A fat lot she cares for me—and I've no use for her!" Sometimes she would resort to tears. If my mother suggested meekly that she could perhaps come on Wednesday instead, Flo's face would flush, she would roll her head and spit out, "You know perfectly well I'm busy on Wednesday!" Under no circumstances would Flo gracefully allow her weekly habits to be disrupted, and my mother would invariably retreat and cancel her plans. This, in turn, would result in yet another unpleasant scene when my father learned that his wife had again been defeated by the incorrigible Highlander from along the street.

Year after year Flo sat there behind our kitchen table on Tuesday afternoons and unburdened all her woes upon my mother's shoulders. She was hardly the most even-tempered person in the world. Flo fought with virtually everyone— indeed, the only reason she did not fight with absolutely every- one was that some, like my mother, did not choose to fight. Flo seemed to think that people went out of the way to insult her, or "slam" her, as she used to say. She always contrived to transform a compliment into a "slam." And my mother would sit there unhappily, trying neither to hurt Flo nor to condemn the person who had "slammed" her. It was the same every Tuesday until death parted them. Flo would talk and have her tea and scone—and suddenly she would hear my father's car rattling up the driveway, she would squeeze out from the bench in a great panic and try to be out the back gate before my father closed the garage doors. It was not that he would be angry to find her still there. Flo merely recognized, quite rightly, that the master was home and his supper should be on the table at the appointed hour.

Wednesday was a half-holiday for the shops, including Collister's where Isabel worked as a cashier. She sat like some mighty queen high up on a balcony along the far end of the building, where she received little metal containers carried magically up to her on an electric cable, and which she returned just as magically with the correct change to precisely the spot from which it had been sent. One of the wonders of New Westminster it was—and it was operated by Miss Isabel McCulloch, who always graciously condescended to wave to us from her throne on high whenever we entered Collister's Drygoods Store. But Flo always spent Wednesday afternoons with her sister. Thursday was choir practice night and Friday—Friday was market day. We patriots of Burnaby, it must be admitted, were profoundly affected by New Westminster's market day.

In summer my sister, brother and I would vie with each other for the privilege of going to the market with Flo. The winner would scamper down Fourteenth and wait patiently for the 9:15 streetcar on Kingsway. It was a nerve-wracking experience since Flo was always late. You would stand there hoping and praying that she would arrive before the streetcar. You heard the rattling rumble of the car approaching around the bend and you knew that this time, for sure, Flo would miss it—but no, there she was, racing down the half block with her short little steps, her two shopping bags swinging wildly across the elbow of one arm, the hand pressing her great broad-brimmed hat squarely upon her head, while the free hand stuffed her greying hair beneath it. You stepped out onto Kingsway so the car would stop—and you would hesitate, to give Flo time to scramble aboard, panting and puffing and madly rummaging through her purse for a ticket or a dime, whichever she came upon first. By the time she found it, you were ensconced on the wicker seat and Flo came staggering along the aisle and squeezed you right against the window. And the streetcar would swing and sway down the hill and up Columbia Street to the market, where the next great adventure began.

It always seemed so cool in the half-light of the market as you followed along behind Flo through the drudgery of the handiwork stalls—tatting and knitting and sewing and crocheting and all those other strange things the country women did on the other side of the river. But then you went down one floor where there were magnificent vegetables, and Flo's bags would begin to bulge, and down another to the fish and meat stalls. Flo went always to Mr. Hall's stall where she would examine various fillets of cod or sole or salmon. Mr. Hall would hold a fillet in one hand while Flo inspected it minutely, as he chewed a piece of gum, or perhaps it was a candy, his soft, cleanly shaven, pink jowls working, his receding hair neatly combed, his bored eyes wandering to his waiting customers. Then he would turn the fillet over, the procedure would be repeated and if it was finally judged to be fit for Em's supper, he would slap it into a piece of wax paper and wrap it up in an old copy of the *British Columbian*.

There were flowers and plants on the next floor down. By the time we left it, daisies or violets or primroses peeked out over the edge of Flo's two great handbags. But the bottom floor was easily the best. Pigs and sheep and cows and horses and cats and dogs and chickens and ducks. Flo probably never descended to that lower floor, at river level, unless one of us was with her, though she enjoyed the beasts as well as anyone. As I petted or stroked or stood in awe she would stand patiently, massively, laughing softly in her whimpering manner, pleased with my pleasure while we visited the stalls. And finally we would climb back up all those stairs and Flo would buy me a bag of homemade candy before we burst again into the summer sunlight.

Then down Columbia Street, Flo taking up half the sidewalk—but even then she was not finished. She would stop at Spencer's Department Store or Nixon's Stationery or maybe Collister's—and certainly at the Window Bakery where she would add at least four boxes of goodies to her burden, two boxes tied together with string, looped through the fingers of each hand. The Window Bakery was always the last stop. There was no room for more.

Flo invariably caught the streetcar home at Sixth and Columbia, right below the great draughting room where my father worked. The Twelfth Street car, which would carry her back the way she came, virtually to her front door, was certainly more convenient, but she always—always—took the Sixth Street car which meant that when she alighted at Thirteenth or Fourteenth Avenue, she had to walk six or seven blocks to her home, part of the way over rough dirt roads and the irregular path through the field on Douglas Road. She did, of course, stop at our house en route, whether one of us was with her or not. She would appear in the middle of Fourteenth Avenue about 11:30, pansies and daisies and primroses protruding from her bags, Window Bakery boxes hanging heavily from her fingers. In the very earliest days she used the old asphalt sidewalk, but once, when the grass and weeds began to grow over it, she came upon a snake sleeping there in the sun. Flo was not the type to scream. She had no qualms in displaying displeasure or anger publicly, but sorrow or surprise or fear were meant to be suppressed. Perhaps she jumped a little; certainly she stopped abruptly, backed away and turned around to Douglas Road. Never again did that sidewalk feel the weighty tread of Flo McCulloch's feet, snake season or no snake season. The road was safer.

At any rate, she would place her bundles down beside the kitchen table, squeeze herself into the bench, never taking off her hat lest her hair should tumble down, and bitterly describe the latest "slam" against her person. Flo McCulloch Doran was the champion of the acid tongue—but she was sweetness, too. If I came in from play, as I invariably did when Flo appeared, my mother would turn upon me in half-anger, shift her weight to one leg, tip her hips slightly, place her hands akimbo and ask with as much mock exasperation as she was able to muster, "Well what do *you* want?" If I said, "Nothing," she would answer, in the same tone, "Well take it and *go!*" and Flo would giggle softly behind the kitchen table. Or sometimes Flo would answer for me in a simpering, childish voice, "Something to eat," and she would giggle softly and reach down past the daisies and primroses and bring out a bag of homemade market candy. I would get shooed out, Flo's tongue would again become acidulous, and just before my father appeared for lunch she would rumble out the back gate and down the street to Kingsway.

Proud, stubborn, sensitive, viper-tongued—and kind, sweet and faithful—Flo and Isabel. We always spent Christmas and New Year's Day with them, alternating between the two households, though the festivities actually began on Christmas Eve. Em always delivered the McCullochs' parcels that evening and we always hoped that he would arrive before we had to go to bed. As far as my brother and I were concerned, we were not interested in the gifts Em brought us, since they were always the same: long, heather-coloured, hand-knitted stockings which reached to our knees and folded down to reveal two blue stripes. All nice little Presbyterian boys wore short pants at that time and I suppose those stockings were a blessing

to my mother, though they could hardly be looked forward to
with anticipation by her sons. We wanted to stay up to see Em
and all the beautifully wrapped parcels he brought. The trouble
was that Flo never quite got things ready on time, no matter
when she started. If Em arrived by ten in the evening, it was
indeed remarkable. More often it was midnight; but if he did
come earlier, my brother and I could see our presents, so
small and soft and plainly wrapped. We knew what was in
them. My sister and my mother always got larger parcels and
they were always much more beautifully wrapped than ours.
They smelled nicer, too, since there was invariably at least one
bottle of perfume or rose water or bath salts amongst them.
Actually, when the lovely wrappings were removed the next
morning, their presents were not any more exciting than ours.
There would be things like underwear and slips and aprons and
"goonies." Goonies were very popular in our community. I
suppose the word was a Scotticism for "nightgown," since that
is what they were. A goonie looked like a great flannel tent
with a hole for the head and two sleeves that reached the
wrists. Flo's were particularly tentlike since she made them
herself and undoubtedly used herself as a model. They were
always about four sizes too large for my mother. But they were
very popular in the days when coal and wood furnaces would
invariably burn out during the night. On a cold winter afternoon I have seen Mrs. Healy wiggle in anticipation and say in
her vigorous manner, "Ooo, it'll be good to get into my nice
warm goonie tonight."

Em's nocturnal visitation, however, really marked the
beginning of the festivities, and the next morning we would
open our presents, then prepare either for the McCullochs'
arrival or for our visit to the house on Kingsway. My father
drove us down about five in the afternoon, but only Mi-cah
and Em would be ready for us. Isabel was off in her room
dressing herself carefully in her usual artistic manner and Flo
was madly rushing about the hot, untidy kitchen in a soiled

cotton dress, her face flushed, her hair completely dishevelled. If you were foolish enough to enter that hellish kitchen, any number of Isabel's numerous cats would scurry out of your way, a thousand disagreeable odours would assail your nostrils and you knew you could never enjoy your dinner. As it turned out, however, you were always able to consume a considerable amount since, by the time the meal was served, you had very nearly succumbed to starvation.

In the meantime, we would sit in the living room with its great bay window facing southward—and full of the bric-a-brac Isabel had collected over the years: pine cones, driftwood, shells, bulrushes, pampas grass, assorted bells and a wonderful disc-shaped gong which resonated softly through the house when struck with a leather-headed mallet. Isabel's paintings covered the walls, and in the corner by the bay window was a huge grand piano with beautifully carved legs and untuned strings. Isabel would finally appear and sit there, looking so clean and polished and stylish, with her favourite cat, Skeezix, on her lap. We were very uneasy about those cats, especially about the dozen or so that seemed to scurry away in all directions when we ventured into the kitchen. Every year we would discuss amongst ourselves the possible number of cats Isabel had in her menagerie, but even my mother and father avoided asking such a question since it would certainly be considered far too personal—indeed it would probably be considered a "slam." At best, Isabel would reply only with haughty silence and a displeased look upon her handsome face, and at worst, she would snap back viciously at the unfortunate questioner and remain aloof for the remainder of the evening. Such subjects were avoided, while Flo rushed, panic-stricken, about the confusion in the kitchen.

We would finally be called to dinner. The sliding doors leading to the dining room would be opened and Flo, now dressed a little more neatly but still "fair trauchled," would serve the soup, which was always only lukewarm and covered with a thin film of grease. My mother helped, but Isabel just sat there at the table like a queen being served by her minions. She was really a cool customer. Then good old Em would carve the turkey right on the great long dining room table painted royal blue—and surrounded by Isabel's birch trees blowing in the wind—and we would forget the kitchen and eat prodigious quantities of turkey, creamed corn, Brussels sprouts and potatoes, followed always by jello with a dab of whipped cream on top, unfortunately never sweetened with sugar. There was never any question of alcohol or wine but, as a special treat, we drank Canada Dry ginger ale with our dinner. The adults had tea and Christmas cake and shortbread and talked of Perth and Dundee and Oban, and finally everything would be cleared, the table moved and we would have games: musical chairs, dice, dominoes, bagatelle and blow football. And always it was the Scots against the Canadians, to wit, Flo, Isabel and our parents against the three children and Em. Whether you won or not, there were prizes for everyone—maybe a model car or a set of dominoes, and my mother always got a water-colour painting with a little calendar attached from Isabel.

In spite of delays and cats and odours, it was the most wonderful evening of the year. And it was all repeated a week later except that we waited patiently for the McCullochs to arrive at our house. We would finally hear Em's Willys Knight chugging up the driveway; he would stop at the front door and gently lift Mi-cah from the back seat. If it happened to be raining, she would have an old felt hat of Em's stuck on top of her head, but always she had a fine, soft, purple shawl thrown over her wasted shoulders. She would be placed on our couch, nodding and smiling sweetly, her eyes sparkling. After dinner we would find some Scottish music for her on the radio or on records and she would lie there and weakly beat out the rhythm with her twisted hand, and she would look absolutely happy. Once my father had a bagpiper come in and march up and down the hall for her, and once Mrs. MacLeod was invited to sit beside her and speak Gaelic to her. Such a strange scene it was to see two close family friends sitting there speaking so softly in such a strange tongue.

These were the greatest evenings of the year for us, as they probably were for the McCullochs. Em and Flo never seemed to go away for a holiday or go out to dinner or a picture show. In the summer we might all travel by tram, ferry and bus to West Bay for a picnic, and often Em would drive us over to the Capilano River on a Sunday afternoon for a sandwich or an ice cream cone at the Tomahawk Restaurant, but the McCullochs had few outings. And their customs never changed—not even by death. Mi-cah died in 1932, but nothing, other than her absence, was different from before. Even when we three children grew into adulthood, not one of the daily, weekly or annual customs varied in the slightest. Flo and Isabel's pride, their sensitivity and their acid tongues perhaps became more acute. Their family was forever intertwined with ours in a strange relationship of turmoil and pleasure.

three

Bowen Island was on the other side of the world, a hundred light years away, even though, by my father's watch, it took the *Lady Alexandra* just one hour to get there. It seemed so very far away partly, I suppose, because transportation was difficult and partly because it was a major problem in logistics to move the family to the island. "An awfie slaister," my father used to say, though he unfortunately never spelled the word for me. But it was my mother who bore the brunt of the burden. My father, it is true, had to make a special trip to Vancouver to stock up on his fishing tackle at Lipsett's sporting goods store, but it was my mother who had to calculate the amount of clothing, groceries, bedding, towels, pots and pans, coal oil and a thousand other items she must buy to keep a family of five for two or three weeks. Some items might be purchased on the island, but you were never sure, and the prices of the articles available there were enough to frighten a Scottish housewife half to death.

At any rate, this exciting pile of holiday paraphernalia accumulated in our dining and living rooms over a period of a week or so. On a Thursday evening my father would start to pack and on Friday evening the task was completed, just before the truck labelled Edmonds Coal and Wood backed up our driveway, Mr. Emerson Doran at the wheel. The bedroll, the cabin trunk and a heterogeneous group of suitcases were piled in amidst the remnants of Nanaimo coal dust and planer ends; then Em and my father would drive the ten miles to the Union Steamship Company dock in Vancouver. We were supposed to be asleep by the time they returned, but we seldom were. Next to Christmas Eve, this was the most exciting day of the year—in fact, the Saturday trip to Bowen Island may have been every bit as exciting as Christmas itself.

Our faithful driver was back again the following morning, this time with his Willys Knight, and in half an hour we were bouncing over the railroad tracks in front of the Union dock, from which you could see the *Lady Alexandra* leaning slightly on the pilings, her decks swarming with picnickers and holiday-makers. We would scramble aboard and watch anxiously till the winch on the foredeck lifted our trunks and suitcases up from the dock, over the side and down through the hatch into the hold, all in one wild, swinging motion. There were always frightened jumps and screams when the whistle blew at five to nine—and at nine o'clock on the dot the dock mysteriously parted from us and the great adventure had truly begun. Out past Burnaby Shoal and the Narrows and along the wooded shores of West Vancouver to Point Atkinson, where you knew you were just halfway there, and in half an hour the *"Alex,"* or sometimes the *Cynthia* or the *Celia,* would turn into Snug Cove, where there were always ten thousand tanned bodies waiting on the dock.

Snug Cove. It was an abomination to my father and, consequently, to his family. It was crammed with noisy people, there was a store, and a dance hall where people drank on Friday and Saturday evenings and, my father suspected, probably on Sundays too. But we had to dock in Snug Cove. It was the only way you could get to Mount Gardner Park. The *Lady Alexandra's* winches would hiss and rattle as the supplies and baggage were unloaded, and from somewhere amidst the throng on the dock, Percy Dorman would detach himself. He always seemed to recognize our baggage. He would wrestle it over to the carrier fastened to the rear of his jitney, we would all pile in, and soon we would be pounding up the hot, dusty hill and into the trees where the road was always damp and shaded, and where you could smell the moisture of the forest and the odour of alders. There was peace and silence here except for the pounding of Percy's old touring car, careening around the bends of the singe-track dirt road. Up and down and around for three and a half miles—past the one-room schoolhouse and the farm, past Lake Killarney and the Grafton Bay road—and you knew you were almost there. In a moment you could see the green waters of McKechnie Bay down though the alders and the ferns; the jitney would sputter up the last hill and through the gate that was never closed, marking the boundary of the Gibson and Wells property. You would burst out into the sun again, past the orchard—and there was Elephant Rock still lying lazily below—past Alf Wells's house, and Percy would pull his old bus to a halt amidst a cloud of dust in front of the store, or a little farther if you were going to a cottage on up the hill.

This was Mount Gardner Park, the domain of Mr. James Gibson and Mr. Alf Wells. My father first came upon it about 1925 when he went there to supervise the construction of the Dominion Government wharf. He had lived in a tent that summer, but it had seemed such a beautiful spot that he returned with his family for many years. There had been some mining activity in the area before the arrival of my father, for up the hill and through the trees there was a deep shaft, perhaps twenty-five feet square, cut through solid rock and extending downward forever into darkness. There was a smaller shaft down closer to the water and the remains of a little railway and a rusted boiler. Not far away, on a cliff overhanging the water, a huge bunker of logs was slowly rotting away. Someone probably lost his shirt on the mine, but whoever the unfortunate gentleman was, he left behind two or three houses: the big lodge named Rest-a-while, Ivy Green and

Alf Wells's house. Those three, at least, were old rambling buildings, even in our earliest days at Mount Gardner.

Perhaps the store, too, was a relic of the mining days. With three floors, it was Mount Gardner's skyscraper. The middle floor, at road level, was the store and kitchen, the top formed the living quarters, and the lower one, down the bank, was an ancient dance floor consisting of sagging boards, a wind-up gramophone and a record of "The Waters of Minnetonka." The name of the store was Do-drop Inn, a name that irritated my father considerably since it assumed the Canadian mispronunciation of the word "dew."

Probably it was Gibson and Wells who built the other cottages—Reverie, Ivy Green, Brentwood, Ocean View, Braeside and two others whose names I no longer remember. In later years, another was constructed and referred to always as the Doll's House. They were little more than a shelter over your head for when it rained, and even then they were not at all reliable. There were no ceilings, the partitions were meagre, the floors bare and full of knotholes through which you could see the open ground, there was no plumbing and no electricity. A veritable wonderland to us all—except to my mother who, in addition to the other inconveniences, did not relish cooking over a miserably small wood stove in a dwelling little better than a shack.

All this lay in a small bay bounded by McKechnie Point to the east, near which Dr. R. E. McKechnie had a cottage, and Eastman's Point to the west, where Dr. Mack Eastman had a cottage. To the south towered an unnamed peak and to the north, across the water, were Keats, Gambier and Hut islands and the mainland. It was a fairyland on the other side of the world.

To my father, it was a fishing holiday. You would hear him creeping around the cottage before dawn, then the quiet, careful scrape of the closing door and the rattle of his Gibbs Stewart spoon on his fishing rod. And if you listened carefully, you

might hear him padding along the boat float, then the echo of
the rowboat round the bay as it slid into the water, and the
click-click, click-click of the loose rowlocks. If you looked, you
could see the muscles of his forearms rippling as he pulled and
the little swirl of water with each stroke of the oars and you
knew that he was alone and happy in the silence of the dawn.

After breakfast he would often sit on the verandah and read
a pulp magazine, usually a western, about cowboys and bank
robbers and cattle rustlers and sheriffs. I do not think he read
them anywhere else but at Bowen Island and he always said
that he would not let his children read such junk—but he read
them, and so did we when he was not around. But my father
would not sit there for very long. He might help us find some
sea worms on the piles of the dock so we could fish for shiners,
or he would find some work to do. My father worked for the
pleasure of working, from the satisfaction he gained from it. He
would borrow a long cross-cut saw from Alf Wells and cut up
logs on the beach and split them into stove wood. We would
usually help him—perhaps with a little persuasion—and certainly we would carry the sticks up to the cottage on a wooden
stretcher that Alf had for the purpose. Or he would replace a
broken board on the verandah or repair the rotting steps leading to the cottage. And if my father worked for pleasure, my
mother did so out of a sense of duty. It was no holiday for her,
she used to say, though there is no doubt that she enjoyed it. In
the afternoon she would come down to the wharf and fish for
shiners with us and then we would all go to the beach and play
on rafts and logs, and swim. My mother always brought some
cookies to the beach, to be eaten after our swim. She called it a
"shivery bite" since by the time we got out of the water the sun
was behind the mountain and it was cold.

After supper we would all go fishing in one of Alf's clinker-
builts. Two would sit in the stern fishing, my father would
row, one child sat on the thwart behind him and the last
would lie on the floorboards right inside the nose of the boat. It

was nice in there with your ear just an inch from the water. When a little breeze came up, the ripples would tinkle pleasantly against the boat's prow. Mount Gardner was a place of sounds—and it was a place of sounds because it was a place of silence. It was a rarity to see a power boat or an aeroplane. In the morning there was not a sound to be heard but the ripple washing gently on the rocks. When the sun came up, you might hear a piece of seaweed burst or the rocks crackle as they dried. Through the day, the westerly would whistle through the trees and you could hear the waves breaking on the rocks and crows cawing and seagulls screaming. At eleven o'clock, no matter where you were, you would hear Percy's or Lisle Davis's jitney roar into the settlement, and a cloud of dust would rise into the trees. But in the evening there was complete silence again. You might hear the scuffing of feet on the dirt road and the murmur of voices or the soft pad of rubber-soled shoes on the dock, and when it was dark there would only be the wash of the ripple on the beach or the pounding of a diesel tug far over by the mainland or the happy laughter of Eve and Mary and Ellen and George in the cottage on Eastman's Point. If you woke up at night, the water would still be washing on the beach, but you might hear the steps of a deer on the rocks or the soft pad of its hooves on the grass outside your window. It was silence that made sounds at Mount Gardner.

In the earlier years all the cottages would be filled, though later on there might be only two or three occupied. Hugh and Dewar Cook were always there as well as a few immigrants from Vancouver, and we had paper chases through the woods or hikes to Lookout Rock, or we would play tennis on the court that some anonymous but resourceful individual had built halfway up the mountain. It was on a flat ledge, with cliffs dropping downward on one side and rising upward on the other. The soil was deep and damp and fertile and huge alders grew in abundance, touching each other far above you, even over the tennis court. Beautiful lush ferns splayed out everywhere beneath them. It was always damp and cool and dark up there. Someone had cleared a dirt court from the woods, and at the start of every year we had to rake away all the leaves and branches accumulated from the previous fall. After that, my father would establish one corner and then pull out a long cloth tape measure from his back pocket. Tape measures were just as common as plumb bobs in our house; it was therefore not unreasonable that my father just happened to have one when we cleared the tennis court. He knew the dimensions and, as he measured it off, we would follow with lime which we had obtained from Alf, along with a net.

That tennis court was remarkable, not only because of its peculiar position in a dark grove of alders halfway up the mountain but also because there was a huge cedar stump, in the middle of one back court, that must have been a thousand years old. You could chip little pieces from the outside, but it was solid beneath the surface. The stump actually added to the fun since the rules allowed you to aim for it from the other end, while your opponent tried to prevent you from hitting it. Surely there was not a tennis court in the entire world in a stranger setting. It was beautiful, too. You could walk amongst the old grey alders where last year's leaves would rustle and your feet would spring from the spongy soil; it was cool and quiet and peaceful, and you could smell the odour of the woods.

At least once a year my father would organize a stream-fishing expedition. We would dig worms and prepare rods from sticks and pieces of line to which we would attach shiner hooks. We would set off with a lunch for the three-mile hike along the road to the schoolhouse just above Snug Cove and fish our way upstream. My father loved that outing. He used to show us, usually unsuccessfully, how he guddled for trout at Esperson Farm with Tom Lawrie when he was a child. We would catch small trout—which darted out from beneath the roots of trees—all the way up to the large pool in a deep cauldron just below Trout Lake. My father's eyes lit up when he first saw that pool. He always believed there were big trout there, though it was difficult to fish. Once he climbed carefully around the cliff, stood on a little ridge of rock and dropped his line down with great expectations. He leaned over to see where his hook was, his backside struck the cliff behind him and he bounced off into the pool. Somehow he landed on his feet with water up to his chest, and the cauldron echoed with childish laughter. But he stood there stubbornly and fished for a while— and he never caught a thing in that big pool.

It was a great event when Flo and Em came to visit us. They always came on a Sunday—and surely it was the only Sunday in the year that Flo was not sitting there with the sopranos in the Gordon Presbyterian Church. They would appear in the jitney at eleven o'clock, Em carrying a huge, battered suitcase filled with clothes and food and goodies. Flo always brought lots of goodies. She would sit for the rest of the day on the verandah or on the beach with my mother while Em went fishing. In all the years he visited us he never once caught a salmon, even though he would spit on the hook and announce with a gravelly laugh that it was just for luck. The westerly blew too hard in the afternoon to fish from a rowboat. One year though, my father took Em to a more sheltered spot to try cod fishing and they came back with three large lings and the most tremendous red snapper I ever saw. Em was really happy that day. He would then put on his bright green bathing suit that went right up over his shoulders and had a little skirt. Over the years it developed a few moth holes, though it served him well. He would step into the water, gasp and scream at the coldness of it, splash water on his arms and face and plunge in to breast-stroke in a wide circle while Flo giggled softly on the beach. Em was ready for a "shivery bite" after that and then it was time to leave—and we were always very sorry to see them go.

Isabel sometimes came up for a day or so, but she was not as much fun. She would usually just sit on a rock and sketch, dressed in a floppy sun hat and a perfectly white dress with a brightly coloured tie around her neck. She always said the scenery reminded her of the Western Highlands, though it was not quite so beautiful. When my father took a photograph of her, as he frequently did, she never looked at the camera. She would gaze forlornly and artistically out towards the horizon.

Over the years, others would occasionally visit us—the Stuarts of Pitlochry, the Gibsons of Glenboig or Jessie Ingram of Galashiels with her friend Phyllis Saunders. And once Mr. Fennel, the principal of Edmonds Street School, came to congratulate my sister when she won the Governor General's Medal, which pleased my father greatly. But generally it was a quiet spot, far from the noise and bustle of the city.

Alf Wells, of course, was always there. He was the owner-in-residence and consequently the absolute monarch of all the land and the inhabitants thereof between Eastman's Point and the gate at the border of the McKechnie property, which he ruled most benignly. He was born in Ontario—or "Ontawrio" as he used to say—though the date of this event would be pure conjecture. He always seemed to be a very old man, though this could be an erroneous observation. Perhaps he looked a trifle ancient to childish eyes because he was small and frail and because he walked in a rather jerky, unsteady manner, his knees always partially bent to compensate for the bow in his back. But even though he looked frail and bent, he had a wiry, tenacious strength that allowed him to chop prodigious quantities of wood, anchor the float in the spring, beach it in the fall and shift his rowboats in and out of the storage space beneath the store.

When he lifted his stained felt hat to scratch his head and survey the weather, you could see his hair was still brown and fine and neatly parted on the right side of his delicate, narrow head. His skin was white where his hat shaded him but below it was a dusky tan colour with little blue veins on his cheek and a blue haemangioma on his lower lip. His teeth were yellow tinted except for his two upper canines which glowed a solid gold when he smiled. Alf always wore a khaki shirt open at the neck just enough to show a trace of woollen underwear, and on top of that, the open waistcoat of an old suit, the unpressed pants of which he wore daily.

Alf Wells probably worked very hard in the fall and spring, but summer was a lazy season for him. You might hear him rattling around in his tool shed near his front gate or you might see him pushing a lawn mower over his rolling grass or slowly and deliberately repairing a broken board on his boat float. And one year he could be seen quite frequently in the cool shade of the open storage space beneath the store, repairing his Johnson Sea-horse. Alf Wells had the first outboard motor I ever saw, though I never saw it in the water. He had it mounted there beneath the store, its cover off, and he would tinker away endlessly while the saliva dripped in shiny strands from the curved stem of his pipe. Occasionally you would hear the motor cough and sputter for a couple of cycles and a wisp of blue smoke would float up from behind the store, but Alf's mighty Johnson Sea-horse never really ran.

Alf's other child of the industrial revolution was a motor car of ancient vintage and indeterminate make. And like his Johnson Sea-horse, it never ran, at least not in my time. It was always propped up on four blocks of wood in a garage beneath the lodge. Alf's car, however, was a wonderful place for children to play. You could spin the narrow wheels beneath their square mudguards or bounce around on the horsehair seats beneath the high, cloth-covered roof. But the greatest delight of all was to press down the plunger of the horn just outside the driver's seat. That delight, however, always produced a terrible raucous screech which invariably brought several adults to chase us out of Alf's magnificent motor car.

The place where you were most likely to find Alf Wells in the summer was in his woodshed, halfway between his house and the store, overlooking the water. The shed was made of

corrugated galvanized iron. Sometimes you would find him
sharpening his axe on the worn old grinding wheel, which he
could spin around at a remarkable rate, the sparks flying madly
down to his feet, his glasses on the end of his nose and his pipe
hanging down from the middle of his mouth. Sometimes he
would chop a little wood, but he spent more time in that
woodshed than seemed warranted, judging from the general
absence of sound emanating from it, so much so that we used
to think he had a bottle of something or other hidden away
there. We actually spent part of an afternoon searching the
various nooks and crannies for specific evidence but found only
a few empties. Alf's frequent presence in the woodshed can
probably be attributed to the fact that it was an ideal spot from
which to observe the whole bay and, more particularly, his
precious boats. The children belonging to the four or five
families who inhabited Alf's realm during the summer were
hard on his old clinker-built boats. They would splash each
other by skimming the oars on the water; sometimes they
would bump into each other and sometimes they would run
up onto Elephant Rock, just between the legs of the recumbent
beast, and scrape Alf's carefully painted hulls. He never shouted
at them or complained to their parents. You would suddenly
realize that someone was watching you and you would look up
at the shed and there was Alf, leaning on the doorpost, puffing
on his pipe and watching, watching—and the water fights
would immediately stop, or you would drift away from Elephant Rock. He just needed to look at you.

Alf always had time to talk, though his range of subjects was
somewhat limited. His world was Mount Gardner. There was
no electricity and consequently no radio. Transistors and the
modern battery had happily not been invented. And I never
recall seeing Alf Wells with a newspaper. It must have been a
wonderful existence. If you cared to talk about the weather,
the Johnson Sea-horse or the deer that stole silently into his
garden at night to eat his apples, he appeared to be most

pleased. And if outside news somehow leaked in from the metropolis of Snug Cove, he was quite delighted to discuss the latest gossip involving the Davises, the Dormans or the Woodses. One of our longest conversations took place in the woodshed where he showed a gang of us how to chop a block of wood by bringing the axe blade down on the outer edge of the block, on a line that would pass through the core, at the same time flipping the blade slightly as it struck. Alf could do it without the least strain of his bent little body. On other occasions you might see him on the road in the evening and he would stop, look out on the water, push his hat back, puff on his pipe and say, "By gollies, by gollies, it's ca'm out there—oh it's ca'm out there." Or if you caught a salmon and took it along for him to weigh, he would dance with pleasure. "Boys oh boys!" he would chuckle through his pipe, "Look at that one, eh!" and he would hop up and down from one bent leg to the other and show his two great golden tusks.

But Alf just did not do much in the summer—little relaxing jobs maybe, like tinkering with his Johnson Sea-horse, keeping a protective eye on his clinker-built navy and discussing such grave matters as the weather with his summer subjects. It must have been a lonely life, yet to us children, he was the luckiest man in the world; he was allowed to stay in Mount Gardner all year round. We never thought of the cold, lonesome nights, the nearest neighbour two miles along the road. His house, though, was certainly more comfortable than the summer cottages he rented out to us city folk. It was a low, two-storey building, its shingled sides always neatly painted brick red, its window frames pure white. It seemed to ramble here and there so comfortably over the rolling grass above the cliff, as if it had grown there along with the old apple and arbutus trees about it. The ceilings inside were low, the hallways narrow and the living room was crammed with old furniture and numerous coal oil lamps. And, like so many places of vivid memory, it had a distinctive odour to it, perhaps of old leather or cigar smoke or, we suspected—though we really did not know how it smelled—maybe even of whiskey.

Alf's garden, like Flo's, had a pleasant air of informality about it. There were a few perennials up against the house, but generally it was rolling grass with apple and arbutus trees, one of which held an old triangular dinner gong with an iron striking bar hanging nearby. We probably annoyed Alf when we sent the resonant reverberations from that triangle echoing around the bay and into his sitting room, but he never said a word to us. Then there was a horseshoe pitch in the orchard, and down by the cliff an old car seat had been hung by chains from a pair of stunted fir trees. You could swing gently there in the evening, only a third old fir, directly in front, preventing you from falling into the sea.

It was a lovely spot in the summer—and we children assumed it was always summer in Mount Gardner. The sun always shone, the warm wind always blew in from the west and there was always swimming and fishing and hiking at Mount Gardner. We never considered that it might rain in the fall or snow in the winter or that the water might freeze solid in the wooden pipes leading down from the dam or that Alf's outhouse might be a trifle chilly. We never considered the possibility that Mount Gardner was a very lonesome spot from Labour Day till the end of June, that Alf Wells lived alone there—though there were actually three or four years when he had a neighbour in McKechnie Bay, half a mile or so along the road and down through the woods. Harry Finlay or "Hawrry," as Alf pronounced it, lived on a houseboat there. It was little more than a shack built on four or five huge logs, one end of which just touched the beach at high tide while the other floated. At low tide the whole contraption sloped steeply downward, high and dry on the beach.

It is altogether likely that Alf and Harry hardly ever saw each other between summers, but to us it was a great delight to walk along the road past Alf's house and down beneath the alders, the ferns brushing our knees, to visit Harry Finlay. You would usually find him sitting on a rough bench on his patio or foredeck, depending on whether the tide was high or low. And if you accepted the fact that Alf Wells did little in the summer, you would have to agree that Harry Finlay did nothing. It is entirely conceivable that he did nothing in any season of the year, though certainly there was always a neatly piled stack of wood on his foredeck and an equally neat stack on the shore above the high-water mark. His inactivity was reflected in his pudgy face; it was always calm, peaceful, serene. Harry Finlay never smiled. Perhaps it required too much energy. Even his speech was lazy. When we appeared, he would turn his head ever so slightly and slowly drawl, "Well, well—what're you up to now?" without any expression on his face. He always seemed pleased enough to see us, but you had the feeling he could take us or leave us. The only thing that vaguely stirred his interest was our red cocker spaniel, Bonnie, whom Harry insisted on calling *Barney*.

It was certainly not Harry's conversation that drew us to McKechnie Bay; perhaps it was the attraction of his houseboat or the relaxing atmosphere—or perhaps it was Harry's right arm, or lack thereof. Harry had no hand; he had a hook, a mean, shiny, iron hook. No one knew how he got it, though there were rumours that he had been in a sawmill accident—if you could believe that Harry ever worked in a sawmill, or any kind of mill for that matter. The hook, at any rate, was attached to a leather sleeve which disappeared under his shirt, if he had one on, otherwise under his long underwear. That hook was a great fascination. It was shiny and polished with years of wear, though we hardly ever saw Harry Finlay do anything with it, mainly because we rarely saw Harry do anything that required either arm. He would sit there, his hook resting on his right knee, his left hand stroking Bonnie's head, and he would say, "Well, Barney, you just look like an old lion." He rarely said much more, and since even hooked arms can get rather boring in a few minutes, we would drift off to the Point or up to take a look through the windows of Dr. McKechnie's abandoned cottage.

Occasionally we would see Harry on the road, ambling along slowly—just moseying along—looking calm and serene, without a care in the world, great broad police suspenders holding his pant legs well above his boots. He should have been singing gently to himself, or at least humming a tune, but walking, I suppose, was enough of a chore for Harry without his further expending energy in song. If it was "ca'm out there," as Alf would say, and the tide was high enough to float his rowboat, Harry might row over to the float, saving himself a climb up the hill to the road. That was the only time we saw Harry using his hook. He had a groove cut into the handle of one oar, into which his hook fitted easily. From the road you could see his short, awkward strokes carrying him slowly out of the bay; he would amble up the dock, buy a few items at the store, relax his weary limbs on the rustic bench outside the door and then mosey off again to his rowboat.

Alf and Harry added greatly to the pleasures of Mount Gardner, perhaps just by exposing us to a different species of animal than we saw in New Westminster or Vancouver or even in semirural Burnaby. And there were others who appeared from time to time, mostly itinerant storekeepers. How Alf ever persuaded anyone to keep shop there for two months of the year is quite a mystery, since there was obviously little profit in it. And there were years, of course, when he could not find a victim. On these occasions we had to rely on Percy to bring us supplies from Snug Cove.

Of those who succumbed to the blandishments of Alf Wells—or perhaps of his partner, Jim Gibson, who lived in town—there was Mr. Bishop, a huge, aging gentleman whose spectacles magnified his eyes into two great grey orbs and whose fame rested in his affability, his candy jars into which he frequently allowed our grimy hands to plunge and his slot machine. Miss Smith was another. She was a middle-aged, wiry type who unfortunately was not imbued with the pleasant indolence of Alf or Harry or even Mr. Bishop. She was cursed with all the imperfections of civilization: cleanliness, neatness and an obsession for work. She made numerous little signs to advertise her pies, cookies and cakes which, though they were indeed most agreeable to the tongue, were purchased by the ladies of the community largely out of pity for their fellow slave. Miss Smith's most lasting achievement, however, was the sign she placed over the picnic table. It was painted emerald green with a neat black border and on it she printed, in exquisite red letters, outlined neatly in black, the legend, "Please place refuse in receptables provided." We really did not know what this meant, but it did not matter since the tables were never used, except to sit upon when we tired of swimming, fishing or hiking. But Miss Smith's sign gained her immortality. It was, after all, the only sign Mount Gardner ever had and it was the neatest, prettiest sign that anyone in our community had ever seen. The only trouble was, we did not need it.

The queen of the storekeepers, however, was Mrs. Leader. For two summers fate somehow gathered together Alf Wells, Harry Finlay and Mrs. Leader, all in that one isolated spot on the other side of the world. She was perhaps in her fifties and, like Alf and Miss Smith, she was small and wiry. Her hair was henna red, her face was a field of freckles, and she always wore a clean cotton dress covered in front by a full cotton apron. What Harry lacked in volubility, Mrs. Leader more than made up for. When she was led, often on purpose, to her favourite topic, words absolutely gushed from her mouth in great torrents, many of them hardly fitting for the ears of fine, God-fearing Scotch Presbyterian children. Mrs. Leader, in fact, was the first lady I ever heard swear.

One day soon after our arrival she was sweeping off the dust that Percy's jitney had deposited on the square of planks in front of her store, as we lounged on the bench. If there was anyone close enough to listen, she could never keep quiet. Her voice was vibrant, her words so clearly enunciated, so fluent. "This place could be kept a lot nicer if it wasn't for that lazy bugger, Alf Wells," she grumbled with gusto. That's what she said. She called Alf a lazy bugger. I do not know whether we were embarrassed or greatly amused at the time, though certainly for me it was a momentous occasion. And she did not stop there. "Why Alf and that other goddam loafer, Harry Finlay, was standing right here last spring," she went on, her anger rising, "an' I says to them, 'boys,' I says, 'why don't you go up in the woods there an' cut me some cedar boughs an' I'll make a couple of hanging baskets for the store.' Why that goddam Alf Wells just puffed on his pipe an' looked up at the trees an' said, 'Oh them boughs is wet—them boughs is wet.'" And she danced up and down awkwardly on bent knees exactly as Alf did and tapped her index finger upward on the end of her nose, wiping off the drop of moisture that always hung on Alf's nostril. "An' Harry just stands there half-asleep with his hand inside the top of his pants an' says, 'Oh them boughs is wet—them boughs is wet.' Why I never seen such two lazy buggers. That goddam Harry Finlay just sits on his ass all year round on that houseboat an' never lifts a goddam hand to help a poor widow."

We told our mother and father about Alf and Harry saying, "Oh them boughs is wet," and we often mimicked Mrs. Leader dancing up and down wiping her nose, but we never mentioned the swear words. Our tongues could not have formed them. Yet, though we never thought of it at the time, our father must have heard them a million times.

From that time on there were never any dull moments at Mount Gardner. If we became aware of approaching boredom, we would drift into the store on some pretext or other and we would say to Mrs. Leader, "Tell us about the time you asked Alf and Harry to cut you some cedar boughs, Mrs. Leader." She would stop sweeping and look up at us, surely knowing how much her story amused us, then her lips would start working in and out and she would finally snap, "Goddammit! Don't remind me of them two. I seen enough of them two buggers last spring to last me all year. Why the two of them was standing right there outside my door an' I says to them, I says . . ." and off she would go in a volley of curse words and invective directed at those two happy old men, Alf and Harry.

Women are not very important in your childhood. Mothers you accept quite casually and people like Flo and Isabel cause a little spark of interest and love, but the Mrs. Leaders of the world, rare as they are, seem to burst upon you and give you joy and a peculiar vibrancy that jars you every time you dream of them. She was perhaps the only heroine of my childhood, but after two delightful summers, she disappeared. Harry Finlay, too, disappeared—to some other secluded spot in some other isolated bay. We missed them both at first when we returned the following summer, and after that they became merely pleasant memories. We did not have the sensitivity to inquire into where they went. Alf Wells remained, growing older but not changing—standing there at the woodshed watching his boats even when we were in our teens, or scratching his head and muttering, "Oh it's ca'm out there—it's ca'm out there," or jumping up and down, his golden tusks shining with pleasure, gleefully chuckling the same old words, "By gollies, by gollies—that's a good one," when we brought him a fish to weigh.

It was, as I said, a fishing holiday for my father, though it is entirely possible that the odours of the alder and the sounds of silence meant as much to him as it did to his children. It must have been something new to him. When he was young, did he have a two-week holiday in paradise? He rowed on the Tay near his home, but he did not have a father to teach him. Perhaps on Corsie or Kinnoull he smelled the odour of trees and stored the sounds of silence in his memory, but did he ever have a holiday, as his children did?

Old men grow older and youngsters mature and wander

away, some to die bitterly in Europe; and none knew the fear
Alf Wells must have felt the night he awoke to find his house
in flames. He escaped, but his brick red house collapsed into an
irregular mound of grey powder spreading beneath blackened
apple and arbutus trees on the scorched grass. Alf moved
around to a basement apartment in the Woods' great yellow
house on the rocks above Grafton Bay. We visited him there in
1945. He was still the same, though he had the fire to talk
about now, and he did so with little external emotion. Shortly
after, we heard that he had died.

Several years earlier, Ivy Green met the same fate as Alf's
house, but the six original cottages, the lodge and the store
remain; the only changes are those of age. The names on each
cottage have weathered away and are forgotten, the paint is
peeling and the steps and verandahs which my father repaired
so often are, to say the least, most unreliable to walk upon.
Many of the great alders and evergreens have been logged away
and the old trails are lost, but you can still pad softly down to
the float at dawn and row your boat out on the calm green
waters and hear the click-click, click-click of the rowlocks
echo round the bay and see the little swirls that your oars make
drifting away behind you. It is unlikely that you will hook a
salmon—which once abounded there—and it is very likely that
you will feel a trifle dated as the power boats skim past you on
their way to Salmon Rock. Physically it has changed little. The
greatest change is that Bowen Island and Mount Gardner are
no longer on the other side of the world.

four

My father was in Alaska when the war began. In spite of the inhuman edict from Ottawa, he had risen in professional rank and about this time became district engineer for British Columbia and the Yukon. The Depression had not noticeably altered our lives. We were aware that some of our friends were forced to work off their taxes by cleaning boulevards or ditches for the municipality, and now and then we would return from school to find a "tramp" eating at our kitchen table, when Flo was not ensconced there. My father occasionally hired one of these unfortunates to work in his garden, but he always grumbled later that the job was not performed thoroughly and thereafter he would simply slip some money into the hands of those who knocked on our door looking for work. An electric stove replaced the old coal and wood burner in our kitchen, much to my mother's consternation since she could never quite accept the concept of electrons running freely around her kitchen in little copper wires. And the old ice box in the basement succumbed to a refrigerator, freeing my father from his weekly trip in the Nash to the Pacific Coast Terminals for a block of ice.

At Christmas my father's increasing importance in the engineering community was reflected in a constant stream of gifts from business acquaintances, a practice understandably frowned upon in future years. At that time, however, we viewed with

anticipation the sight of a great automobile slipping up through
the pillars at the foot of the driveway. We would listen for the
knock on the door, accept the offering and wait patiently for
our father to return from work to open the most recent gift
from our mysterious benefactor. There were fancy letter
openers, expensive wall barometers or thermometers, silver
salvers and serving dishes—and a veritable flood of alcoholic
beverages. The elusive business acquaintances—perhaps they
were private dredging companies or contractors or hardware
suppliers—could not have known my father well. The bottles of
Scotch and rye and gin were quickly hidden away from the
eyes as well as the reach of the adolescent children of the
household, knowledge of their ultimate destiny carried to the
grave with my mother and father—all but one lonely bottle of
Scotch per annum. When one of us developed a head cold, my
mother mixed an unpleasant concoction of Scotch, water and
grapefruit rinds which when drunk, she firmly believed, would
destroy the evil cold virus. Mustard plasters upon the chest and
warm turpentine rubbed firmly into youthful ribs were also
some of her magic potions, though neither of these produced
the diffuse feeling of well-being of the Scotch-laced remedy.

The advent of my father's rise in his profession also brought
a more frequent mention of politicians in our household,
though only in relation to my father's work. He never dis-
cussed politics. The party for whom he voted was privileged
information, fit for no one's ears but his own. The dredging of
rivers, the formation of dykes, the construction of docks, the
control of waterways, brought politicians to his door. In retrospect, they all seem to have been Liberals, though perhaps this is
understandable since that party seemed to have been in power
since time immemorial. My father often talked about Tom
Reid, Ian MacKenzie and, later, James Sinclair. It is no more
than coincidence, surely, that they were all Scots. Tom Reid
was Member of Parliament for New Westminster for many
years and had therefore a great interest in the Fraser River. He
had a farm across the river at Strawberry Hill, and it is said

that he used to raise hell in Ottawa by marching up and down the corridors of the House of Commons playing his bagpipes. This story may have been apocryphal, but it made our little community all warm inside and it endeared Tom Reid to my father, to say nothing of many of his constituents. My father was somewhat more reserved in his feelings towards Ian Mac-Kenzie, who represented a Vancouver constituency and was later minister of defence. This gentleman had a very red complexion—and a red complexion, to my father, was incontrovertible evidence of boozing it up too much. Race was one thing to my father, booze was another. Presumably young Jimmy Sinclair did not suffer from a red complexion, for my father was a great admirer of the North Shore member. In later years I attempted to shake his faith by pointing out, from my offensive store of adolescent knowledge, that the Sinclairs might indeed have recently come from Thurso, far in the north of Scotland, but that the name was originally St. Clair and they were, in fact, nothing but Frenchmen. He merely scowled at me and muttered something about talking a lot of gitter.

My father, as I said, was in Alaska when the war began. My sister was at university, my brother and I in high school. The war itself did not seem to change our lives significantly, though the frequent references of our parents to a trip home were all but eliminated. Certainly the war was not the cause of the barrier that had grown imperceptibly between my father and me. Perhaps it had begun before the war. In the autumn of 1938 my mother told me one evening that my father had just heard of the death of his mother in Scotland and that I should speak to him.

I found him quietly repairing the front steps. I did not know what to say. I felt rather detached over the event. "I am sorry to hear about your mother," I muttered clumsily.

He did not look up. On his haunches, surveying the rot in the lower step, he answered resignedly, "It'll happen to you someday."

No more was said. Perhaps he was thinking of the last time

he saw his mother, twenty years ago, and their unhappy part-ing—though at the time I was not aware of it—or perhaps he was considering that his sons would soon be old enough to go to war or that they would soon be leaving home, as he once did. There must have been a myriad of thoughts spinning through his head. But we never spoke of such things; in fact, at that time we rarely spoke of anything. There were no more casual visits to the draughting room, no more exciting esca-pades on the *Samson,* no more bar fishing trips to the mouth of the river. We had drifted apart. It was merely the passage of time and the development of a brash sophistication in a teen-age son, strutting about in his new-found knowledge with which a mere civil engineer in his fifties could not possibly be acquainted.

In the next four years he did indeed see my brother and me dressed in the mock uniforms of the Canadian Officers Train-ing Corps while we were at university. He developed angina over this period, though he continued to work in his garden, occasionally slipping a nitroglycerin pill beneath his tongue and complaining that the garden was getting too much for him.

In 1944 I left my father's home to study medicine in Mon-treal, returning only for summer jobs. But we saw little of each other. My work was mostly out of town and my father tra-velled more and more frequently. Yet when I was home, I had a strange urge to toil in his garden—to cut the wide expanse of grass on the tennis and croquet lawns, to trim the boxwood hedge which had grown profusely around the rustic fence he had built with the sweat of his brow when I was a child, to weed beneath the ornamental bushes he had purchased from Mr. Livingstone out near Central Park so many years ago. And to dig the weeds from his driveway above the pillars. My father had always planned to lay asphalt there. Several times over the years he had surveyed the area, pounding in little stakes to mark the proper level for his proposed blacktop, but it was one of the few projects he never accomplished. Weeds grew along the sides and down the centre between the car ruts, and each year I would root them out beneath the summer sun. It was labour that I hated as a child but which gave me satisfaction as an adult.

Each year my father would visit Montreal briefly during a business trip to Ottawa. I would see him from a distance, arriving in Windsor Station, a weekend bag in his hand, the brim of his felt hat bent unevenly in various directions, only half of his coat collar showing, the strap of his Zeiss Ikon across his chest folding back the front of his coat, his broad shoulders bent. My father was untidy. He did not wear clothes well. He walked more slowly now, and as he approached, his face was paler and thinner—yet when he saw me, his eyes would brighten, wrinkles would radiate laterally from his eyes, and a broad grin would spread pleasantly across his aging face. He had lost much of his vigour though none of his enthusiasm for life. He would relate every morsel of conversation he had had with a travelling mate or he would again rage against the evils of the demon Ottawa. And he would slip a little tablet of nitroglycerin beneath his tongue as we wandered up University Street.

He once visited me while I was living in Philadelphia. He had been touring flood control methods on the Mississippi and had had a meeting in Washington. He wore the same old hat, the same old coat, and the same old Zeiss was slung across his chest. There is not a great deal to do in Philadelphia on a Sunday—except to go to church or visit Constitution Hall, both of which we accomplished. The Hall, so dear to the hearts of Americans, was a cold, sterile place. To us, it was merely a means of occupying a Philadelphia blue Sunday. But my father stood there on the bare board floor before the Liberty Bell, explaining to me in unhushed voice the various stresses and strains that must have caused the famous bell to crack. A guard suddenly materialized, tapped my father on the shoulder and announced sternly, "Visitors are expected to remove their hats

before the Liberty Bell, sir." It is one of the few times I saw my
father at a loss for words. There was an awkward pause and
then he smiled broadly and removed the offending battered old
felt hat. That evening, from high in the airport terminal, I
watched my father walk slowly out to the plane, the same old
hat stuck untidily on his head, his shoulders bent, his coat held
open by his camera strap, and I wondered when I would see
him again.

There was one more thing I wanted to do before I sat down
to grow old. I knew that if I ever returned to the west coast I
would never see the land of my fathers, at least not while I was
young enough to enjoy it to the fullest. The last of my grand-
parents, Harry Murdoch, had died in 1948 and there was only
one member of his generation yet living. I could wait no
longer. Travel to Britain in the postwar years, however, was
still not an easy jaunt. Trans-Atlantic flights were expensive,
and the ocean trip was not only slow and uncomfortable but it
was also a psychological barrier. I do not mean to imply that
the risk of falling off the edge of the world somewhere east of
Newfoundland loomed very large in our western minds, but
the ocean was thousands of miles wide, almost as deep, and our
parents had crossed it, if not in the Middle Ages, at least at a
time so remote that it might as well have been. Such petty
matters as poverty, job insecurity and rationing were real
enough, but it was the psychological barrier that had to be
overcome. I managed to do so, and the only remaining factor
to consider was the expense. A freighter would transport me
more cheaply than a passenger liner.

I boarded the *Dorelian* on a beautiful July morning in 1950,
since that is when the Donaldson people ordered its four humble passengers to board and I was, at that time, in the habit of
obeying orders. They did not tell us that they would not be
sailing until the evening nor did they tell us that we would be
spending three days in Port Alfred, up the Saguenay River,
loading aluminum for Britain. They also apparently did not

feel it necessary to assure us that the *Dorelian* was large enough to cross that frightening expanse of water to our destination. She had, after all, survived the war, and I was aware that the *Lady Alexandra,* which used to carry us happily to Bowen Island, and which was perhaps only slightly smaller than the *Dorelian,* had been built on the Clyde.

After dinner I sat on an unstable deck chair and watched the distant banks of the St. Lawrence slide back towards the west. The great adventure had begun—only to be interrupted suddenly by a rope falling around my body, pinning my arms to my side. I turned my head in alarm, to find the skipper standing a few feet away, holding his end of the lariat and laughing madly to himself. He loosened me without a word and disappeared, still chuckling to himself. I had seen him at dinner and would never see him again. When I described this remarkable event to Mr. Dougal, the first mate, he scowled, shook his head and muttered in his Glaswegian manner, "Godstruth! The man's daft. He fancies himself a cowboy."

But even a mad skipper could not stop me now. Without considering it, I had made the same decision my father had made forty years earlier—to sail across the Atlantic to a new land. I did not know why he had come, which ship he had sailed on nor where he had landed. I knew only that I was going in the opposite direction, ostensibly to study, but in actual fact to see the land of my forefathers and their remnants, to see the origins of both my body and my soul. The delay in Port Alfred was torture to both. We sweltered in that hellish heat as ingot after ingot thumped into the aging hold of the *Dorelian,* but on the seventh day of July we slipped away down the stagnant waters of the Saguenay, heat radiating from the cliffs on either side.

By evening you could feel the *Dorelian* lifting in the waves and you could smell the sea salt and feel the Arctic breath upon your face. And by nightfall black July fog rolled down from Belle Isle, and Dougal sounded his whistle. It was reassuring to

know that he was up there in the wheelhouse. He never spoke
of the war, but the third mate had told us that he had spent
more time floundering around in the icy waters of the North
Atlantic than he had on the decks of his four ships, all of which
had been torpedoed.

Sound your whistle, Dougal. In the distance, there is an answer, a
deep, sombre growl, and from my berth it is comforting to know that
you are up there, Dougal. You will be striding back and forth,
muttering to yourself, the quartermaster calm and quiet. It is not his
responsibility, it is yours. You whistle again—three short blasts. A
pause. Three deep, vibrating throbs answer much closer now. Do you
hear it, Dougal? It is a big one, a great masculine monster it must be.
The Dorelian *sounds effeminate beside it. You are ashamed of our*
elfin whistle, Dougal. You will be cursing again in your Glaswegian
tongue as you sound it again. "Godstruth!" you will be growling.
"Worse than the bloody British Railways." There it is again, Dou-
gal. It is almost on top of us—its mighty testosteroned bellow vibrates
in our cabin—but you are there in the wheelhouse, Dougal, and it is
comforting knowledge. Whistle, Dougal, whistle. And wait—wait—
wait for the answer. It is more distant now, Dougal; you have passed
it. But you will still be striding about restlessly, cursing the Dorelian, *the mad skipper and the black July fog rolling down through*
Belle Isle. You will carry me safely to the land of my forefathers. Let
me sleep now. Blow your whistle, Dougal, but let me sleep. It is
comforting to know that you are there.

The days passed so slowly, and yet, as each drifted away,
there was greater peace in my soul. I read *The Raw Youth*,
leaned upon the rail or lay in my berth hoping wistfully that a
gravol pill would counterbalance the spinning in my inner ear.
But when the weather was fine and my stomach steady, it was
magnificent to watch the *Dorelian*, like some huge rudderless
log, plunge her nose beneath the Atlantic, hesitate for a sicken-
ing moment and rise again, white and green water pouring
from her foredeck. Dougal would appear from his morning
sleep. He would amble absently down the deck, his hands deep

in his blue serge trousers, his greying hair flat upon his skull, his stained teeth protruding slightly from his lips. His collarless white shirt was usually held together by a tarnished stud, but if by some mysterious circumstance the stud was missing, you could see a grey-green spot tattooed into the pale skin of his neck. He would sit on the sooty top of a life raft rather than on the empty deck chair beside me; he would cross one leg upon the other and lean his folded elbows on them.

"Godstruth!" he would mutter disgustedly as he gazed blankly out on the grey expanse of ocean. "I don't know why this bloody submarine wasn't torpedoed. When I think of all the bloody beautiful ships that went down . . ." His voice would trail off and he would shake his head in disgust. Every day he would go through the same ritual, just as Flo performed her daily rituals. "Godstruth!" he would growl. "That skipper's a bloody madman. Reads every bloody cowboy book he can lay his hands on, sees every cowboy picture on both sides of the bloody water."

Each afternoon at four Dougal's growling grumbles were interrupted by the appearance of Bert, the steward. He would slip delicately through the midships companionway, his slippered feet shuffling along the slanted deck, spread wide apart, a tea tray balanced carefully on his fat, upturned hand.

"Beautiful day, sir," he would say as he set the tray on the deck chair that Dougal always chose not to sit on. "'Ave an 'untley and Palmer biscuit will you, sir?"

"Thanks, Bert."

"Mr. Dougal?"

"Godstruth! There's nary a Huntley and Palmer in sight when we've no passengers aboard," old Dougal would growl. "It's all for the bloody passengers."

"Not at all, sir," Bert would answer politely but firmly. "Sparks gets his 'untley and Palmer every afternoon," and he would waddle off down the deck, his sockless ankles bared to the Atlantic breezes.

"Bloody Sparks," Dougal would mutter disgustedly.

"Bloody ship's full of madmen. That Sparks never leaves his cabin till he's in Avonmouth. You'll see the bugger slip off for home with his bag, have his half pint of Bass at The Lamb and when we sail again he'll be back in his cabin and you won't see him again till we're back in Avonmouth."

Day after day those who were less sensitive to the sea sat there on the little patch of deck reading, talking and drinking tea with Dougal in the afternoon, as the *Dorelian* rolled and ploughed her nose beneath the Atlantic, spewing water from her foredeck. Wave after wave, mile after mile, day after day. Britain was indeed very far away—but one afternoon Dougal muttered through his Huntley and Palmer that we would see land tomorrow morning. The moment I awoke, I was on my hands and knees on the berth peering out the porthole. It was there. Low flat land with trees spaced evenly along the shoreline and then a tall chimney in the morning mist. Dougal said it would be Swansea. It was hardly what I expected. But the *Dorelian* bored her way up Bristol Channel, past Weston-super-Mare, and by ten that morning she rattled her rusted anchor into the chocolate waters of the Severn just above Portishead. We were here, two weeks after leaving Montreal, thirty years after my mother and father had last seen this land.

I sat on the deck chair looking out on England. It was difficult for me to believe that I was at last here. Mine was an emotion that Dougal could not appreciate. He was born here. He could never experience the thrill of discovering the land of his forefathers, the very centre of the English-speaking world. He rolled up the deck on the way to his cabin, curious, I suspected, to see my reaction to the land I so longed for. His hands were deep in his pockets, his collarless shirt open, the tarnished green remnants of his stud marking the base of his neck, his flat, grey hair gleaming in July sunlight. "We've missed the bloody tide into Avonmouth," he grumbled. "We'll have to sit here all day, and bloody Sparks won't get his Bass till nine this evening." He ambled off to bed.

Dougal, you are an old grouch and I will be sorry to leave you. You growl and grumble, but you enjoy the roll and plunge of the ship and the wide expanse of the sea. You were tense that night long ago when cold black fog drifted down through Belle Isle, but you sensed accomplishment when you slipped safely by that great freighter and plunged out into the clear morning sunlight past Newfoundland. You know the Dorelian *will always lift her nose, you love to see her dip and plunge and you love the lonesomeness of the Atlantic—and you must feel the same deep satisfaction when you sight the landfall in the channel as my father did when he completed the pillars at the foot of the driveway. You do not enjoy lying dead here at anchor, Dougal. You have no use for this—but I do. This is where my world began, a few miles north of here it is true, but this is my historical present, Dougal. It has been mere legend until now. Sitting here on the little square of deck in the warm morning sunlight, I can see the lighthouse at Portishead and the rolling hills above the cliffs. There is a caravan up there. A dog barks somewhere near it and a faint cloud of blue smoke puffs into the air, as if Alf Wells were up there tinkering with his Johnson Sea-horse—but it is a hay mower. It moves slowly off now and the sound of its motor finally reaches my ears. It is beautiful, but it is more than that. The prairies are beautiful, the Rockies are beautiful and Bowen Island is beautiful—but this is Lyonesse, a hundred miles away, and there is magic in my eyes, Dougal.*

We slipped into Avonmouth on the evening tide. Sparks was the first down the gangplank, resplendent in his white turtle-neck and officer's blue jacket, his duffle bag over his shoulder. Dougal winked knowingly at us and nodded towards the receding figure of the wireless operator. Four somewhat unsteady passengers followed him to The Lamb where we saw him drink his half pint of Bass. I would miss Dougal.

A cousin and an aunt on my mother's side of the family met me at Paddington. They had first chosen as their colonial relative another Canadian passenger from the *Dorelian* since he was wearing a straw hat with a colourful band about it. Assuring my relatives that not all Canadians wore prominent hats, he directed them to me and I met the Murdochs. They drove me to their home in Enfield. My aunt and uncle, of course, were Scottish, but my cousins were English as hell. "This is my cousin," one of them said as she introduced me to her tennis club crowd, "we've only just found him." English as hell. It was comforting to realize that one had been lost and was now found again. My father, were he here, would have remarked upon the accents but would thereafter have accepted them as an unavoidable fact of life, just as I did.

Shelter, however, was more important than relatives. I found a bare little room in Bloomsbury, on Doughty Street opposite Mecklenberg Square and settled in to see the city before I was forced to earn my living at the beginning of August. Every street, every building, every step was laden with history. I sated my soul with it. Read and walk, read and walk. I would not have time to see all of London, digest it, absorb it. How could I ever leave this fascinating city? But there were other relatives in London—another Murdoch aunt, Elsie, with English children—and there was Scotland. England was the heart of our culture, but it was still a foreign land. Scotland was my home.

I wrote a letter. "Dear Uncle John," I began. I had to; there was no other way to address him. He was my uncle and I was his nephew—and God knows what he would think, up there in Edinburgh, when he opened this letter and found himself addressed as Uncle John. I was the only person who could use the term, in the proper sense, other than my brother and sister, but they were five thousand miles away. That was the difference. We had occasionally spoken of him at home, and if I had written him from there, it would not have mattered how I addressed him. Relatives five thousand miles away are really quite impersonal beings, but London was so close to Edinburgh that I almost felt I could drop over to see him some evening after work. I did want to meet him of course. One of the main reasons for my coming to Britain was to see my parents' homeland and the diminishing band of my relatives. But my father's brother? The Murdochs were a gentler race. It was not difficult to meet my mother's relatives—but the thought of meeting Uncle John, my father's only living relative as far as I knew, was awesome. He was a mystery. I knew only that he was nine and my father three years of age when their father died. I had a vague recollection that he had once been married for just a few months before his wife died, and of course I knew that he lived in Edinburgh.

It was, then, with a considerable degree of uneasiness that I addressed him as "Uncle John" and asked if I could visit him in mid-September, a month from that date. His answer came a week or so later, written in an old-fashioned hand similar to my father's—and at the bottom left-hand corner of each page, below the last line, he had written the first word to appear at the top of the next page. I had seen this before in old letters of historical interest and had always been fascinated by it. This seemed to make Uncle John even more old-fashioned, but it was a quaint little habit which pleased me at the time, though the general tone of the letter could best be described as reserved. He could put me up in his flat, he said, and he added a word of warning, which I did not know how to accept. "Don't let these English put sugar in your porridge," he said. "Scots use only salt."

On the fifteenth day of September I walked to King's Cross and was soon humming northward towards the land of my ancestors and my fateful meeting with Uncle John. There is a border, you know. You can feel the difference when you cross the Tweed and a few miles farther north you cross the Eye and you see a sign pointing to Eyemouth where my mother used to visit Hastie Collin and her cousins. There is the first faint stir of familiarity and nostalgia. But how can it be nostalgia if I have never been here before? By five o'clock I am in Edinburgh and climb the steps from Waverley Station to burst upon the wonders of Princes Street. Is that the castle? It is not impressive from here. And the gardens and the floral clock and Walter Scott's monument. I put down my suitcase and dally for a

moment. Delay the confrontation with Uncle John. Drink in
the sights and sounds of Scottish voices. Is this home? I was not
born when my mother and father were last here—nor Flo nor
Mrs. Healy nor the Stuarts. Probably Flo was never here. She
was from the west. Is Uncle John living somewhere in this city?
Where is Comiston Road? Ask a policeman. A streetcar carries
me up through Morningside—Morningside, where Mrs. Healy
was born, or did she just live here? I will have to write to her—
up through Morningside to Comiston Road. The conductor
said he would call me when we reached Number 89. Why do I
secretly hope he has forgotten? I sink down in my seat. I am
too conspicuous. He might conclude that I have departed. No,
he stops the car, comes right out into the aisle and shouts, "89
Comiston Road," looking me straight in the eye. It is there all
right, across from a chemist's shop, a four-storey building, grey,
square, cold and gloomy—and somewhere up there sits my
Uncle John. There are times when one must face reality.

The brass name plates of the tenants were fastened to the
weathered stone. "John A. Morton," one said. It was true; there
really was a John A. Morton. I really had an Uncle John. In
Burnaby he was little more than a figure in a fairy tale. Standing there on his doorstep in Edinburgh, I finally knew that he
was real. There was no question of running away to find a
room to remain anonymously in Edinburgh, but there are
times when it is difficult to face the unknown. I was about to
throw myself on the dubious mercies of a strange uncle. I felt
like David Copperfield, or that other poor kid somebody wrote
about—Robert Louis Stevenson it was, in *Kidnapped*. Whatever
his name was—was it David Balfour?—he got into a frightful
mess with his uncle and was sent off to the colonies, which, I
suppose, would not be the worst of fates, since I had just
recently come from one. David Copperfield and R.L.S.'s friend,
however, were just kids. I was twenty-eight, it was 1950, and
with a degree of courage unknown to my ancestors of Gallowmuir and Elgin in 1745, I pulled the bell handle. I heard a

distant tinkle, not an electrical tinkle but an old-fashioned mechanical tinkle. In a moment the front door of the flat seemed to move—perhaps it was the wind—but no one appeared to welcome me. I pulled again and again and the same thing happened. Was I meant to enter? But if I did and was not meant to, would I incur the wrath of my Uncle John? Timidly I turned around in the desperate hope of succour—and there it was. The chemist across the street was standing at his window, waving me to enter the flat. I suppose, from my suitcase and my clothes, it was obvious to him that I was a stranger from another planet. I waved back feebly and pushed the wagging door.

It was a stairwell. A thousand steps and a winding metal bannister twisted up and up, and at the very top I saw a small figure. By the time I reached the second floor, I knew he was my father's brother. He was short and broad-shouldered, he wore the same lines on his face as my father, and had the same receding hairline. There was a difference, though; he was neater than my father. He wore a well-pressed suit, a white shirt, a maroon bow tie and a perfectly manicured moustache. The other difference was that his face was impassive. My father would have smiled broadly and welcomed me enthusiastically. Uncle John did not speak until I was half a flight from him. "Did you not know to come in?" he asked rather gruffly, moving only his lips; then, resigned to his fate, "Come away in." He led the way, his right leg stiffly straight. I later learned that he had been knocked down by a car the year before and had lost all movement in his knee joint. I followed, realizing that it had not been a very good beginning.

It was a rather cold, bare flat—a sitting room, a dining room, one bedroom and a kitchen—and much neater and cleaner than my father would have had it, had he been a bachelor. Uncle John eased himself into a large, soft chair with his back to the windows which looked down to Comiston Road. He bent his left knee, but his right leg was stretched straight out onto the carpet. He filled his pipe, lit it and asked about my trip, my family and my work, all the time holding me steadily with his expressionless eyes—dissecting me, analyzing me, judging me—ashes occasionally spraying up and then floating down onto his waistcoat as he spoke through his pipe. I had seen my father do the same thing. Though I was not invited to sit down, it seemed reasonable at this point to do so and I did, without any overt sign of objection from my uncle.

His evaluation of me was still very much in doubt when, in half an hour or so, he muttered somewhat peevishly, "Well, this is my night for bools. We'll away down to the green." It was not until he had limped over to the hall closet for his bowling ball that I realized where we were going. He put on his double-breasted trench coat and black Homburg and we slowly ambled down Comiston Road and up a side street to the green where his cronies were awaiting him. Perhaps they were just kind to him that evening. Perhaps they let him win only because his newly discovered nephew was with him—or perhaps it was my lucky night. Whichever it was, Uncle John not only won a victory, he won a thrup'nny bit. The joy a Scotsman experiences from monetary gain is so universally recognized, it would be foolish for me to deny, or even to ignore, the fact that Uncle John was now in a much more animated mood than heretofore. He smiled and chuckled and laughed as we slowly made our way back to 89 Comiston Road, his "bool" swinging happily from one hand, his cane grasped tightly in the other, his thrupence resting safely in his pocket. He described his philosophy of the game, the science involved and his strategy in the recently concluded match as if I were one of his old cronies, and when he finally hung away his coat in the hall, he muttered through his pipe, almost absent-mindedly, but certainly proudly, "I'll have to remember to put that thrupence away tomorrow."

We seated ourselves in what were to become our regular chairs, Uncle John turned on his battery-powered radio and, just before Big Ben tolled the hour of nine, he sprung the cover off his gold watch. "Thirty-two seconds late tonight," he muttered in that tone which I grew to know so well and which I was never sure was an expression of concern or of pride. Most likely it was pride, since Uncle John often interested himself in such minutiae and since the loss of thirty-two seconds in his day could hardly be a matter for concern. There was no doubt that he was proud of that watch. The moment the news was finished he turned off the radio, pulled the watch out again, unclipped it from its chain and handed it to me. He must have been contemplating this act as the news drifted up to us from London. "Presented to me by the Arran Estate Office in 1925," he announced—and sure enough, there it was, engraved inside the back cover. This launched him into a number of tales connected with his work as an estate agent, each preceded by, "I mind o' the time . . ." Uncle John, as I soon discovered, was always mindin' o' the time.

From there he expanded into many other subjects, usually unrelated: the universal relief of arthritic pain by bee stings; the uses of sundry patent medicines; the pipe manufactured especially for those who wore dentures; the Royal Scottish Agricultural Fair, which he never failed to attend, no matter where it was held; the history of various Scottish regiments; the British Legion, of which he was a faithful member; and Field Marshal Hermann Goering's personal automobile which, by chance, arrived in town the same day I did. Uncle John was indeed fascinated by Goering's car. He had heard that there were still bullet holes in it and maybe even blood and he was determined to see it, though he cautiously pointed out that he was not sure whether there was a charge for viewing it.

It was remarkable to be sitting there, seeing my uncle before me. At sixty-eight years of age, he was physically an older replica of my father. Many of his expressions were indentical to those of my father, but, in contrast, he was a dapper little man and his speech was slow, deliberate and unmodulated, quite unlike the energetic, enthusiastic, almost volatile speech of his brother. The content of his conversation was also very different. Had I just met my father, he would by now be regaling me enthusiastically, perhaps to my dismay, on his problems with the Fraser River or the measures used to control floods on the Tennessee River or the evils of the demon Ottawa. Uncle John, perhaps because of his state of retirement, was concerned with his watch losing thirty-two seconds or seeing Hermann Goering's automobile.

Another subject which consumed a great deal of time was that of relatives—on both my paternal and maternal sides. My mother's relatives were always most discreet about the various members of their clan. Uncle John, on the other hand, was not one for niceties when they were not called for. "Uncle David was one that watched his pennies," he muttered. "I mind o' the time he took us out to tea in Perth and he said, 'The cakes are a' paid for so eat a' ye want, and those ye don't eat—pocket!' " and he chuckled happily through his pipe.

"Did you ever know the lady my mother's father married after his first wife died?" I asked him.

"I mind o' the time I met her in the post office," he answered in his slow, dreamy manner. "Good day to you, Miss MacGlashan, I said to her and she looked at me, stuck her heed in the air and walked away. Och! Yon Meg MacGlashan—she was an awfie bizzim!"

His meandering recollections continued till well past midnight. They were fascinating, though he made one remark that disturbed me deeply; he announced that he never lit his fireplace—which was the only means of heating the flat—"until the fur-r-r-st day of October" and it was never on after the last day of March. We had been getting on so well, but this was sobering news. Perhaps he made the remark after noticing me shiver. I was dreadfully cold—and I was dying, slowly dying, of hunger. I had eaten a good breakfast about seven that morning, but I had not had a bite since, nor had I been offered one. My parents, I thought to myself as we departed for our respective bed chambers, will at least receive some solace in their sorrow, knowing that their son succumbed in the land of his ancestors. They need not be told that his wasted body was found frozen in Uncle John's kitchen. Ah yes, the kitchen. He offered me his bedroom but in the last few months I had laid my head in so many strange little rooms that the cot in the kitchen was perfectly acceptable.

I lay there with the light still on wondering if I could wait until he was asleep and then slip out to some delicatessen, preferably a warm one. But would they still be open at this hour in Edinburgh? Remember Bill Briscoe preparing his daily sandwich with such care and devotion in Philadelphia just a year or so ago? How perfectly magnificent it would be to have one of Briscoe's liverwurst sandwiches—with a slice of tomato, and lettuce, and perhaps a skim of mayonnaise. Was Uncle John as sound a sleeper as his brother? In my anguish, my eyes fell upon a shelf high above the foot of the cot. There were a number of boxes on it, and one was long and narrow and labelled "Oat Cakes." Was it possible that there were any left, even a mouldy one? I crept down, reached up, opened the lid and slid my hand inside. It was half full. I took one, turned off the light and gorged myself. We used to put butter on them at home, but at this particular moment I did not even miss it. The cake was dry and bitter and delicious—and my mind was guiltless until I had consumed it all, and even then I suffered only slightly. The sleep of the just, the innocent, the guiltless. Perhaps not quite; the memory of the oat cake remains upon my conscience. Forgive me, Uncle John, I was starving.

It must have been many years since Uncle John had prepared breakfast for a guest—indeed perhaps he never had before. He was still as neat as ever, dressed in a clean shirt with short sleeves and resplendent in his maroon bow tie. "Did you sleep well?" he asked as he lit the grate and put a pot of water on to boil. As he set the table, he talked aimlessly but comfortably about anything that came into his head, including his bow tie, of which he was eminently proud. He did not have to tie it, he said; it just clipped on to his collar, and he demonstrated its removal and replacement with a quaint and innocent pride.

"You've got to boil the water first for porridge," he went on, and when that point was achieved, he reached into a small sack of oatmeal with his bare hand and allowed the precious grain to run through his stubby fingers into the pot. My father, my father. I had seen him do exactly this when I was a child, and I was always horrified at his using his hands. I used to wonder if he had washed them—and even though he had, I would have felt better if he had used a spoon or a cup or a bowl. It was foolish reasoning, but children are not noted for their reason and on those occasions I watched my father with filial horror. This long-forgotten memory was recalled only now as Uncle John's oatmeal trickled between his fingers. It was the same pot, the same water, the same sack of oatmeal and the same stubby fingers—and he seemed to treat the oatmeal with the same respect, or reverence, that my father did. They both held it so gently in their hands, as if they were afraid of crushing it, bruising it, as they allowed it to run slowly and carefully into the pot. There was something very personal about the preparation of their porridge. For a moment I thought I was six years old again, sitting on the bench behind the kitchen table, watching my father standing at the old coal and wood stove on Fourteenth Avenue.

And it brought back a faint recollection of something my father called brose. "Aye," Uncle John answered when I asked him about it. "That's the way the farm hands did it at the Muirton." He was stirring now with a well-worn round stick, adding another handful of oatmeal now and then, stirring and adding. "You've got to use a wooden stick," he muttered. "Metal's no good. And you've got to put the salt in while it's boiling. There's no use adding it later. And it's got to be boiled till you can walk on it. I'll have none of yon English stuff here." On he went—adding, stirring, rambling—until he could lift the whole glutinous mass out of the pot in a great blob on the end of his stirring stick.

"There you are," he announced proudly. "That'll keep you going," and he cut the porridge from the stick with a knife into two bowls and limped over to the table. He poured a thick coating of black treacle over his and pushed the can over to me. "I mind my mother used to give us this every morning," he went on between spoonfuls, "and it was the daily breakfast at the Muirton." I considered my stomach—but when one is hungry, nothing else matters.

There was less preparation of his tea. The most remarkable thing was his cup and saucer. Perhaps they were a relic of Fingal who, as far as I know, was the last giant in Scotland. Uncle John's cup and saucer, in Willow pattern, were huge, the cup being about the size of a bowl my mother used for mixing cakes, with a handle added. He poured my tea into a standard-size cup and the rest into his, surely four or five times the volume of mine. This I did not mind; tea for breakfast was an abomination one had to tolerate in Britain. But it was fascinating to sit there and watch and listen as he talked and sipped his great cup empty. And it was the same every morning: porridge and treacle and tea.

After we had cleaned up the dishes, Uncle John limped about the living room dusting little tables, the arms of chairs and the mantel, while I sat at the dining room table writing my father. It was a concession to him. Every week for six or seven years I had written to my parents, addressing the envelope to both, though unconsciously the letter was aimed at my mother. This one would be addressed to and aimed at my father exclusively. Uncle John, however, would not leave me alone. He would wander in, the duster still in his hand and he might say, "I mind o' the time Uncle David came back from New Zealand. His wife was an awfie drinker you know . . ." and he would proceed to describe this great family disaster which, of course, had not been included in the many tales of the Muirton my father had related to his children. I would write a little more, but soon Uncle John would be back. "Does your father still work on the Fraser River?" he asked.

And so it went. Finally he brought his own pad of paper and a fountain pen and sat down across from me, explaining that he was going to write his friend, Mrs. Crawford, to ask if he could bring me for a visit. There certainly was a telephone system in Edinburgh but Uncle John did not have a phone. He sat there ponderously forming his letters, so much slower than my father's rapid, busy scribble, and I wondered if he wrote the first word of the next page at the bottom of the previous one. Every now and then he would interrupt the silence with a few muttered words. "She's a fine wee woman is Mrs. Crawford," or "They've two nice boys, the Crawfords. I'll have to remember to bring them a bag of sweeties," or "I've had this fountain pen for twenty-five years and never once has it failed me. I mind I bought it when the Royal Agricultural Fair was in Paisley."

There were many interruptions, but he finally went off down the street to post his letter. When he returned half an hour later, he was unusually quiet and glum for a few minutes and then he muttered, "An odd thing happened to me at the post box doon the street. I walked up to the box, dropped my letter in and a voice said to me, 'Why hello, Mr. Morton,' and I turned around and by Joves, there was Mrs. Crawford standing before me. It was uncanny—and if she'd spoken a second sooner I'd have saved a penny ha'p'nny stamp." I could not help laughing at his great misfortune, and even Uncle John smiled a little. Despite my fears, I now felt perfectly at home with him. Indeed, I felt quite close to him. Less than twenty-four hours earlier, I would never have dreamed of pointing out to him that since, by happenstance, Mrs. Crawford did not need to answer his letter, she might well agree to split the penny ha'penny with him. "Och!" he answered half seriously. "There's no need to."

We spent a delightful evening at the Crawfords', Uncle John blethering away, as my father would have said, until the small hours of the morning. On other days we toured the castle, where Uncle John proudly and reverently showed me the Scottish War Shrine, or we would wander slowly down the Canongate or along Princes Street talking and window-shopping, his cane tapping the pavement as he went, a leather thong holding it firmly to his wrist. At noon he always had lunch at Binns'. Every day of his life Uncle John had lunch at Binns'. He never missed a day, always at the same table, always with the same waitress. I must have disrupted his regular pattern of life to a considerable extent, but no one could dissuade him from having lunch at Binns'. Nonetheless, I was the cause of his moving to another table. "That's my table over there," Uncle John pointed out to me. "Do you see the old boy sitting there? He's an awfie blether, and he's awfie stuck in his ways. When our waitress goes on holidays, he refuses to come near the place, but her first day back, there he is again, large as life. It's awfie how some people get so stuck in their ways."

In spite of the pleasure we had in each other's company, it was no doubt a relief to both of us when I slipped away by myself to wander through the city or, more often, to the hills—to Salisbury Crags and Arthur's Seat. It was cold and often wet, but it was beautiful there on the hills with the sheep and the ruddy-faced children—who were so scantily clothed and who always seemed to ask the same question: "Have you got the time, muster-r-r?"

But the day I had been waiting for came near the end of my one-week stay in Edinburgh. It came with a strange mixture of longing and fear—longing to see Perth and fear that it could not possibly justify the image I had of it. "I've written to Maymie Padkin," Uncle John said, "and we've to come up on the twentieth." I had planned to go there alone—to walk anonymously along the streets that I already knew so well, to climb Kinnoull Hill, to run upon the North Inch, to lean on the fence of the Muirton and allow my sentimental soul to simmer and bubble and burst into a great mushrooming cloud of emotion. I had, I suppose, expected to experience a tremendous sensuous binge in Perth—and Uncle John was hardly the type with whom one could share such an emotional experience. He was kind and friendly but completely devoid of sentiment. But there was no escape. It was a minor disappointment. There was a bond between us now and I could not expect to go alone. Furthermore, he would be able to show me places I would have difficulty finding were I alone—and I could always go back.

But who was Maymie Padkin? Uncle John informed me that she was the daughter of Aunt Chrissie, one of the fourteen children born on the Muirton in the mid-nineteenth century. I remembered Aunt Chrissie. My father had mentioned her, though I did not know he had a cousin, Maymie Padkin Lindsay, living in the city.

September 20. Porridge and treacle and tea and the train— and Kinross, Dunfirmline, Glenfarg and Bridge of Earn—and no one need tell me that this is the Tay and the tower on Kinnoull, that the stationmaster still wears a frock coat and a tile hat, as he did in my father's day. Here, though, is a modern bus, and it carries us up South Street past Methven and John and George streets, which I know so well, and there is Prince Albert's Monument on the North Inch, and the bridge, and the Tay—where salmon run and pearls lie, according to my mother and my father.

The fact that it was a dull, cold day was of no consequence. I was at last in Perth, the home of my ancestors, my home—and every sight and sound stirred my soul. And essentially I was alone. Not a word was spoken. Uncle John sat silently, stolidly beside me on the bus, staring straight ahead, his right leg stretched down the aisle, his hands resting on the cane which stood erect between his legs. To Uncle John it might as well have been Edinburgh or London or Philadelphia or Vancouver. It was an everyday trip on a bus to him. He did not know how

I felt, though perhaps that is unfair. Behind his inscrutable mask, he might have sensed my emotion but chose not to broach the subject. My father would have reacted the same way, though he could not have hidden his own enthusiasm. We walked up Muirhall Terrace to Gannochy Road—and there was the house where my father was born. Uncle John's cane pointed to the very window. A sign on the gate read Gannochyfold, and I remembered my father laboriously cutting letters from a sheet of aluminum and attaching them, with brass screws, to the gate that he had hung from the pillars at the foot of the driveway. "It's not changed much," Uncle John muttered. "Only the lime trees have gone." Did he not feel any emotion towards the house where he was raised and where his mother died just ten years earlier? I remember when it happened and I can still see my father on his haunches, repairing the front steps as I awkwardly expressed my regrets to him. How did Uncle John feel that day? He would have been sad, but externally he would not have shown it. He would dust the tables and chairs and the mantel and eat at Binns', and his waitress and the old blether who was so stuck in his ways would not notice any difference in him from any other day. And he showed no emotion now as he turned and limped off down the hill to the Tay.

"This must be Lochy Brae, Uncle John," I said, perhaps in a tone which he would reserve for such hallowed spots as the Shrine in the castle.

"Aye," he answered through his pipe.

"And that must be where Miller, the baker, had his shop."

"Aye."

"And that's the Sawmill Stream?" I asked, now on the bridge.

"It is."

He did not even seem surprised at my knowledge of the town.

"And where is Woody Island, Uncle John?"

"Around the bend a bit," and he pointed upriver with his cane.

My father repaired his boat here and rowed my mother up the river and tied up to that little float over there. The river is clear and brown and perhaps there are pearls amongst the stones.

"Could I see the North Church, Uncle John?"

"Och, we've nae time for that."

"Could we go past Sharpe's School?"

"Och, we've nae time for that."

Perhaps I resented his lack of understanding, but he could never destroy those precious moments when we hesitated on the the bridge across the Tay with the North Inch—where my father played rugby in his youth and where my mother walked with Harry Murdoch and her sisters on a Sunday afternoon—stretching off to the distant borders of the Muirton.

Another bus carried us through the town to Cherry Hill and the Lindsays. It was just like a Scottish home in Burnaby; there was the same hominess and the same habits, the same expressions, the same food. My father's cousin, however, had something that was lacking in Uncle John and, to a lesser extent, in my father. She had a deep interest in the family and in the past, and she recognized the same in me. Immediately after lunch her husband, a great angular seed-potato farmer, appeared with a pencil and paper. "I've to make a list of all the things you want to see in Perth," he announced. I was afraid to look at Uncle John. "Och, we've nae time for that," he had said so often. He would be bored. He just liked to sit and blether.

Uncle John was correct to some extent. We had little time, but we drove about in David Lindsay's Austin and we saw Perth Academy and Sharpe's School. A sexton opened the doors of the North Church for us and I sat in the pew where my father's family had sat and I saw the choir where stern old Harry Murdoch had sung and kept an eye on his daughters. At the Muirton, the present tenant, Mr. Clarke, welcomed us.

"Welcomed" is hardly correct. He tolerated us. He was a canny little man, pear shaped, sharp featured, with a cap on his head and trousers that clasped his ankles just above his boots. He stood with his hands inside his belt and looked somewhat askance at three members of the family of tenant farmers who had preceded him. But he pointed out the barns and byres where my father played as a child, and the old house, which Uncle David rebuilt because he believed it vibrated, and the Toll House on the Dunkeld Road and the little cottage where my father's Uncle John lived with his two sisters, Chattie and Lizzie.

It was late in the afternoon before we reached Wellshill. Here, Maymie said, was the family ground. On it stood a monument stretching high above all the rest. It had a great square granite base and a long marble spire, but more remarkable were the inscriptions on three sides of the base. It recorded the deaths of every member of the family, in various corners of the world, from John in 1880 to David in 1937. It was all there before us on that cold September afternoon. Who were these strange ancestors—this John and his fourteen children, all born on the Muirton Farm? Some names were vaguely familiar. I had heard my father speak of his wealthy Uncle Andrew, but why, if he was the eldest child, had he forfeited his birthright to die in South Pasadena, which the stone stated was in "Calafornia"? John, the second son—my father's Uncle John—I remembered as a bachelor living with his two sisters. And William, the third son, died in Callao, Peru? I remembered my father telling us of an uncle who died in Peru after being bitten by a snake. Could he be the subject of this exciting tale from my childhood? And here was James, the sixth son, who died in 1891 when he was forty and his son, my father, was three years of age. Had he died three years earlier, the pillars would not have been built at the foot of the driveway and I would not have existed. It was all there before me, written in stone, on that dull, cold September day in 1950.

As we rattled home to Edinburgh, Uncle John looked straight ahead, his eyes unfocussed, and, half dreamily, he allowed his recollections to tumble slowly forth. "Maymie's father was a minister and awfie keen on croquet . . . Uncle David had a green at the Muirton where we played . . . I mind o' the day we heard that Uncle William died in Peru of a snake bite . . . My mother's father died of a burst aorta . . . I mind I had to ride my bicycle down Lochy Brae and into town for the doctor, but by the time we got back, Grandfather was dead. . . ." It is strange that my father told me the same story with himself as the bicycle hero—but I said nothing. Uncle John enjoyed his recollections and he enjoyed his visit to Perth, as I did, but he was not capable of conceiving the emotions in my soul when I at last saw these sights so familiar to me as mere names, or legends, in my childhood. He could have no conception of the fascination the stone in Wellshill had for me. He had lived here all his life; these relics were too familiar to him to be of any interest. I had the singular good fortune of being born five thousand miles away, of being raised upon legends—and of ultimately seeing with my own eyes these very legends. It was like stumbling into King Arthur and his knights riding out of Lyonesse.

Just a week after I had rung his doorbell at 89 Comiston Road with great trepidations, I said good-bye to my Uncle John, knowing that we were both sorry to part. I took the bus to Glasgow to spend a few days with my mother's eldest sister, Isa, and returned unhappily to London. I knew that I must see more of Scotland and of Uncle John. Indeed, we corresponded regularly during the winter months. There was a difference now though, compared with our August letters. He was no longer a gruff, old mysterious uncle. He was warm and frank and personal. I could see him sitting there at the dining room table, carefully forming the letters with his ancient fountain pen, writing the first word of the next page at the bottom left-hand corner of the preceding one—and venting his wrath on the English. He reminded me again that the English do not know how to make porridge, he blamed the English because I had spelled "Aberfoyle" with an "i" instead of a "y," and when I told him I had been to a party on a Sunday, he replied, "Of course that is the English out and out." The English, he said, always had to call upon a Scottish regiment when they had a dirty job to do, and when I told him I had lost two shirts at the laundry—a great disaster in my penurious state—he answered, "That's English laundries for you. I've gone to the same laundry in Edinburgh for twenty-five years and never lost so much as a button." Dear old Uncle John; his letters were a pleasure.

It is depressing to be in London when your roots are in Scotland, but I worked and gradually realized that though London is not family, it is history and literature. That is not why I came, but it was here before my eyes, and for the first time in my life the importance of my profession began to fade— and for a moment this frightened me. But I walked and walked and let my soul absorb London. Why even Boadicea is here, down by Westminster Bridge. She stands metallically in her chariot with blades upon her wheels, just as my grade school teacher once told me. And up the street is Whitehall Palace where the Stewarts held court, a hundred years before Prince Charles's feet tramped the North Inch and the dusty road from Perth. And do you know Samuel Pepys? My mother used to tell me that Harry Murdoch was his great admirer. You can stand in Salisbury Court where he was born or you can walk up Crutched Friar's Street where he lived, or stand sadly in the bombed shell of St. Olave's Church where he sat on the Sabbath in the Navy pew. You can sit in Johnson's home and drink a pint where he and Boswell drank. You can even drive to Theobald's Park and touch the Temple Bar. A boy from Burnaby can stand beneath the arch through which Johnson and Boswell walked arm-in-arm, two hundred years ago. You can bus to Hampstead and touch the bed where Keats coughed out his lungs and stand beneath the tree where he lay and heard a nightingale sing. Or so you like to imagine. And is it possible that there are still lamplighters? I stood in Doughty Street in disbelief as November dusk approached. And it is true. Old Leerie is here in London. He has just passed the old house with a blue plaque upon its wall, Number 48, a few doors up from mine. "Residence of Charles Dickens, 1837-1839," it reads.

But Dickens is a distraction. He reminds me of my room across from Mecklenberg Square. Number 29. It is the darkest, dingiest, dustiest little room I have ever been in, but most of all, it is the coldest room I have ever been in, now that winter is here. I have never been so cold or so hungry in all my life. That is why Dickens reminds me of my room. He always wrote about poor little wretches who were cold and hungry and miserable and motherless and fatherless—but not uncleless or auntless. I was very, very cold and very, very hungry that winter at 29 Doughty Street, though the knowledge that Mr. Dickens was my neighbour provided just a little touch of comfort in my agonies.

Perhaps he would call on me. I would drop a shilling in the slot of the gas grate and he could sit in my chair close to the hissing flame and burn his shins while the remainder of his body shivered.

Would you care for a handkerchief to wipe your frozen nose, Mr. Dickens? Did you know that Mr. and Mrs. Donald Stuart of New Westminster used to give me your books for Christmas when I was a child? I did not read them immediately, though I did when I was older. Of all your characters, Tom Scott was my favourite. Whatever caused you to create a boy who walked upon his hands and tapped at windows with his feet? Remarkable.

Would you care for a piece of cheese, Mr. Dickens? No—I ate it all just last night. Let me place my empty tin of Balkan Sobrani tobacco upon the grate, Mr. Dickens, and I will heat some water and you can have a cup of Camp Coffee. It is vile stuff, but I like it because my father and mother used to drink it at Bowen Island. I like it, too, because on the label there is a Highlander sitting in all his glory with an Indian servant standing obsequiously behind him.

Anything tastes good when you are hungry, Mr. Dickens. Take last week, for instance. There is food rationing here and my mother sent me an overseas food package. I gorged myself until there was nothing left but the Camp Coffee and a huge slab of cheese. What kind was it? I don't know, Mr. Dickens. I know nothing about cheese. As a matter of fact, I dislike cheese. I have been away from home for so long that my mother has completely forgotten how I abhor it. But last night, Mr. Dickens, I was very, very hungry and I broke off a wee bit, about the size my father used to place in his mouse trap. But the cheese did not taste nearly as bad as it did at home, where there were many other more palatable things to eat. As a matter of fact I nibbled a bit more and before I knew it, I was slashing at it like mad, just as your friend, Oliver Twist—but no—he was a polite, well-mannered child, was he not, Mr. Dickens? He would not have slashed at his cheese—or his porridge. Pardon me. My point, however, is that I crammed that whole great wedge of cheese into my mouth and let it roll gently round my taste buds and it was perfectly delightful. That is why I don't have any for you to taste tonight, Mr. Dickens. But have a cup of Camp Coffee, and I'll put another damned shilling in the grate.

And when you leave, I will crawl into my flannel pyjamas, pull on two pairs of knitted woollen socks and wrap my woollen sweater about me, and I will roll myself into a wee ball and in the morning I will still be rolled up in a wee ball and my joints will be frozen so solid that it will be painful to straighten them. There will be a kipper and fried potatoes for breakfast. Tea for breakfast is a cross one has to bear in England, Mr. Dickens. You have been to America. You know the delights of a good cup of coffee in the morning.

I could no more sate my soul with the sights of London than I could sate my stomach with cheese on Doughty Street. There were a limitless number of antiquities outside London. The English claim they are authentic, but how can anyone believe that Hampton Court, which was built by Cardinal Wolsey— or so Miss Vert at Edmonds Street School told us—is still standing there so magnificently? How can you believe that all those beautiful carvings in wood—of flowers and foliage and birds—

were carved, not only by human hands, but by *one* human hand, that of John Evelyn's protégé, Grinling Gibbons? There are similar carvings all over the city and up into Scotland, and the English tell us they were all done by the hand of Grinling Gibbons. There is not a soul in Burnaby who has either the skill or the patience or the endurance to do work like that—unless it is my father. The gentleman in Petersham was more realistic. He was digging a post hole when I asked him where I could find the parish church. He looked up at me and do you know what he said? He said, "You must be from Vancouver." There was no doubt that the grave in the churchyard was that of the captain who sailed into Burrard Inlet in 1792, just as the *Lady Alexandra* does now. You come upon places like that so casually. One day my Uncle Andy was driving me to his flat in Battersea when he suddenly stopped, backed up a bit and said, "Come in here. I want you to see something." It was a Lambeth churchyard and on a stone was inscribed, "Rear Admiral William Bligh. 1754–1817." He saw our coast with Cook when only Indians lived there.

But there were a million fascinating spots. We drove to such places as Shaw's Corner, Chalfont St. Giles, Stoke Poges and Granchester. My neighbour, Mr. Dickens, perhaps never heard of these villages. Londoners are notoriously ignorant of their shrines—or, if they are not ignorant, they are at least unappreciative of them.

Do you know who lived in Chalfont St. Giles, Mr. Dickens? John Milton. I am no great admirer of him, mind you—just as I am no great admirer of you, Mr. Dickens, with all respect—but you, after all, are my neighbour. Mr. Fennell, our principal at Edmonds Street School, for some long-forgotten reason used to speak of Areopagitica. *I never understood it, but I loved to hear him say* Areopagitica—*and perhaps he loved to hear himself say it. Milton was married at St. Giles Cripplegate, just above St. Paul's. Sometimes I go down there and sit on a section of the Roman wall that was exposed by German bombs during the war just a few years ago, and look sadly upon the* shell of St. Giles and its tower, held together by pipe scaffolding. You can see all the church spires of London from there, most of them built by Christopher Wren. Milton was married right there where I sat, Mr. Dickens, and that day out at Chalfont St. Giles, I stood in Milton's cottage.

Stoke Poges? You don't know Stoke Poges and I will wager that you don't even know Gray and his "Elegy," Mr. Dickens. You have been spending too much time writing those books the Stuarts used to give me for Christmas. I could not condemn you for not knowing that Mr. William McKeown of Burnaby South High School one day sat before us and read Gray's "Elegy" with the trace of a tear in his eye. That was the day I realized that there were other things in this world than football. Gray was buried there, Mr. Dickens; I saw his stone and I thought of Mr. McKeown and Burnaby.

Granchester is up by Cambridge, Mr. Dickens. I had no idea where it was until that day. In fact I had never given it serious thought. But my uncle and aunt drove me to Cambridge and I saw Saffron Walden and Audley End and Magdalen College, so well known by none other than Mr. Samuel Pepys. Do you know him? When was his cipher transcribed? 1825. You must have known his diary, Mr. Dickens. But Granchester was after your time. We stopped there for tea. From mere whim, we ordered honey and were served without ceremony. You see, Mr. Dickens, there was this fellow named Brooke who wrote a poem about Granchester during the first war. "Stands the clock at ten to three and is there honey still for tea?" That's what he said, Mr. Dickens, and we enjoyed our tea very much.

But I must be boring you. You must understand, though, that I am a starry-eyed patriot of Burnaby where there is no local heritage of literature nor history. I did not expect to become so awed by England's past, but I have, Mr. Dickens, and I hate to leave it now, so near the end of March. I have even learned to love my cold, miserable room on Doughty Street. This is partly because you are my neighbour. The cold and the hunger are nothing compared with the pleasures I have had in London. Why, you can sit in the gallery of any theatre in London and listen to Laurence Olivier and Vivien

Leigh or Michael Redgrave or Emlyn Williams for a mere shilling or two.

Remember me, Mr. Dickens. Think of me on Saturday nights when those magnificent Welshmen hold their weekly dance in the hall behind our homes on Doughty Street. You can hear the music only faintly during the evening, but at midnight—or is it one o'clock—you are awakened and the roofs for blocks around are virtually lifted from their ancient moorings when those Welshmen sing their national anthem. I never heard it before I came to Doughty Street, Mr. Dickens, and I never understood their strange tongue, but the beauty of their voices is one of the more magnificent sounds I have ever heard. I am about to set out for Lyonesse, a hundred miles away, and I am sorry to leave you—but remember me on Saturday evenings, Mr. Dickens, when the Welshmen sing "Land of My Fathers."

It rained in Lyonesse. It rained a great deal in Lyonesse—but I walked for miles and miles through Devon and Cornwall and back again, occasionally accepting a ride in an automobile, occasionally being forced to ride a bus in order to reach a hostel before nightfall. There were wonders we never saw in Burnaby or New Westminster or even in Vancouver. There was Stonehenge, there were castles and cathedrals and rolling English hills and waves crashing upon the rain-swept rocks of Land's End. But there were also people—about whom my friend, Mr. Dickens, could write: ghosts and spirits, town criers and monasteries full of abbotts. There were adventures every day, and I returned from Lyonesse, damp and dirty, with magic in my eyes. But it was the end of March now and in two days' time I had to be on the train to Edinburgh. I knew I would enjoy it yet I hated to leave London and all those lovely villages, just as I had hated to leave Scotland last September.

five

I have developed a strange ambivalence and feel guilty about it. The English are our sworn enemies and yet I love their cities and villages, their art and history and literature. I feel I am leaving civilization for a wild, ragged country where the lassies are wind-blown and the tongue is coarse. Scotland seems so far away now. As the train speeds northward, I suspect that I will change again, but I am depressed. The weather does not help. "At the back o' seven," as Uncle John would say, it is raining in Edinburgh and I wonder why it is not snowing.

I found a little space in Miss Grant's boarding house not far from the streetcar line and by the back o' nine I stood again at the door of 89 Comiston Road, across from the chemist's, where I had stood six months earlier, wondering what manner of man my uncle was. I knew now. He was as gruff as ever and just as dapper in his white shirt, maroon bow tie, dark suit and waistcoat, his hair and moustache neatly trimmed. Uncle John was always the same. And he was always there in his flat so neatly dressed that, no matter when you called, it seemed he was always expecting you. In the many times I visited him that spring, he was out on only one occasion when he had gone to a British Legion meeting in Glasgow.

We managed to settle down in our regular chairs just before he clicked on his radio, pulled out his watch as Big Ben sounded the hour, and announced that he had lost another thirty-five seconds. He slouched down in his chair with his stiff right leg stretched out almost straight with his body and listened, without expression, to the BBC news. The Stone of Scone, removed from Westminster Abbey by Scottish Nationalists, had not yet been found by the evil English, who had originally stolen it from the palace across the Tay from the Muirton Farm. In Korea the King's Own Scottish Borderers were advancing on the 38th parallel, and in London Clement Attlee, it was said, was attempting to suppress a revolt in his cabinet, headed by Harold Wilson. Uncle John sat there stolidly, listening and staring dispassionately ahead, as if I were not there—but he turned off the radio five minutes before the end of the news, perhaps to be a little more sociable, perhaps to save a little battery power.

He shifted slightly in his chair and said, "Well, I've had my sixty-eighth birthday since you were here last. I'm in fine health and I've my mother's stomach powder to thank for it." Here we go again. I didn't say it aloud, but that's what I thought. "My mother got the recipe from Grandfather Taylor and she never had a day's illness as long as she took it. I mind she used to get it made up at old Tulloch's on the High Street. The chemist across the road makes it up for me . . ." It was as if I had never been away. I had forgotten about the stomach powder. It used to stand on a shelf below the clock in our kitchen on Fourteenth Avenue, in a little brown bottle which was just transparent enough to let you see how much powder was left. There was a label on it from Bews Drug Store on Columbia Street. My father would remove a teaspoonful, put it directly into his mouth and immediately wash it down with a glass of water—and a grim expression would appear on his face. It must have tasted bad but my father would never show it, other than by a momentary tightening of the lines on his face. We knew it was his mother's stomach powder, we knew it had a bitter odour, and we knew our father was somewhat bilious when he plunged my mother's teaspoon into the brown bottle labelled "Bews Drugs."

It was peaceful sitting there talking to Uncle John, but I also wanted to see more of the country and walk on the Pentlands and Arthur's Seat and Salisbury Crags. That April you could not even see them for the mist and rain and snow. London was fascinating in any weather, and as I trudged each morning beneath the castle walls and up the Vennel Steps, I cursed the day I came to Scotland. But Uncle John was a pleasure. I would visit him once or twice a week and each time it was the same. We would stretch out in our chairs and he would ramble on endlessly. There was no problem in communication. He would slide quickly from one subject to another, almost always touching upon some incident that I had already heard from my father, or some person with whom I was familiar.

Such was the case with the Lawries. "Jim Lawrie was the finest shot I ever saw," he muttered, apropos of nothing, in his slow, deliberate drawl one evening, as if he had the whole night before him. "I mind o' the time we sent the dug into a thicket after a hare and they both came out together and ran up the brow of a hill—and Jim shot the hare right oot the dug's mouth." He remained expressionless as I laughed heartily, took a couple of puffs from his pipe, and went on in the same tone. "An' once he felled a pigeon in a tree an' before it hit the ground he brought down a hare that rose with the sound o' the gun. Oats is the finest food there is, you know. I even bait my mousetrap with it. I mind a shepherd at Esperson who lived all year on oats an' hare's blood soup. I hear the English drink nothing but cocktails. I only tasted o' one in my life—an' I didn't like it. They're insidious things; before you know it, you're away. The Crawfords wanted to go to a dance the other night so I told them I'd come an' look after the boys—but they'd better be back by 1:30 or there'd be no one there . . ."

Uncle John could ramble on forever, and not only with me as his audience. He later mentioned, in passing, that he had arrived home at 3:30 in the morning, after sitting with the Crawford children. A few astute questions revealed that the Crawfords did indeed return home by the 1:30 deadline, but old Uncle John had just sat there talking till almost 3:30. His conversations were both interesting and amusing to me, but after dancing Scottish reels till 1:30, the Crawfords must have been pleased to see the last of Uncle John. Even when I got up and moved to the hall for my coat, he would find some pretext to carry on the conversation. "That's an awfie auld Mackintosh you've got there," he said one evening as I struggled into my one and only coat, and worried about how I would get up in the morning. "I've got one just like it here in the closet." I could hardly depart while he rummaged about looking for it. When he finally found it, he held it up for my inspection—and absent-mindedly put his hand into one pocket. "Hello!" he said, in the most surprised tone that I ever heard from my Uncle John, "Hello! There's a pair o' gloves in the bloomin' pocket. By Joves, I'd wondered where that pair o' gloves had gone. I mind o' the last time I wore that coat . . ." I escaped half an hour later.

Do you know that it snowed on the first day of May in Edinburgh? This was a great disaster for the lassies of the town since, it seems, they were in the habit of washing their faces in the May dew on Arthur's Seat on the first day of the month. Actually it was a blessing, for they were already a wind-blown, hamely lot; May dew and Arthur's Seat would merely weather them more. The precipitation and the temperature kept them in their homes, just as they kept me in my room or in Uncle John's flat. But late one afternoon in the second week of May, when I was reasonably certain that the Arctic icecap had descended permanently over the land of my ancestors, I stepped out to the street in the Old Town and discovered that the sun was at last shining. I looked southward and saw the crags. Have you ever seen the late afternoon sun strike the buff cliff of Salisbury Crags? It was like a huge iceberg hanging over the city, and I was drawn irresistibly towards it.

There was suddenly an invigorating sense of spring in my soul. Sheep grazed and chewed and turned their heads to watch me warily as the wind parted their wool into great deep clefts till it showed yellow at its roots. I walked far up that smooth, green slope to the edge of the crags and looked down over the city of endless chimneys—where there were thousands of wee wifies preparing dinner for their families. I could see the Braid and Pentland hills and Arthur's Seat. I could see people walking, sometimes in twos or threes, but more often a solitary form on the skyline. Scotland is a land of skylines with solitary figures silhouetted against them. Let me be one. It was cool and fresh and clear and I could smell the sea-salt blowing westward from the Isle of May. And down below there were children playing in the ruins of St. Anthony's Chapel above St. Margaret's Loch.

"Muster-r-r, have you got the time?"

"It's a quarter of six," I answered and they laughed uproariously. They had never heard it put that way.

"Dinna shout, Jean, he'll think yer daft!"

"What's your dog's name?"

"It's nae my dug," Jean answered.

"Och Lassie! It is yer dug. Yer afraid the man'll make ye take yer dug frae the park."

And as I walked past St. Giles Cathedral, three dirty little children rushed down in the opposite direction and, without breaking their stride, they all simultaneously spat on the sidewalk. I looked down and saw the Heart of Midlothian set into the pavement and I heard the older girl shout in exasperation, "Och! Ye'll nae get yer wush, Johnny. Ye didna' sput in the centre."

Suddenly I seemed to hear things and see things that must always have been there. I no longer had to worry about the weather. I was warm and dry and everything pleased me, and I felt at home. I remembered the little story old Mrs. Gregory once told me. I did not understand it for a long time. A lady, visiting a friend, noticed the family cat sleeping peacefully on the couch. "It looks at 'ome," she said in her broad Scottish accent. "It's no' a 'Tome,'" was the reply, "it's a Tabbie." I suddenly felt at home and everything was pleasing.

I began to visit somewhat distant relatives in little towns such as Kirkcudbright and Strathmiglo, Burntisland and Eyemouth. Strange and distant relatives out of the past. Sometimes I would walk in the evening out past Corstorphine to Blackhall to visit my mother's Auntie Rachel, and she would count for me. "Fower, fife, seex, seffen, aicht,"—"Aicht" was my favourite—and she would lean forward in her chair and tell me how Harry Murdoch loved his bairns. She would see him in his bed on the Sabbath morning—"An' there he was, wi' a' his bairns about 'im." Her sweet old face would light up with pleasure. On each visit there were the same tales, and Uncle Jack, slightly exasperated, would say in his slow drawl, "Och Rachel! Ye've told him that a thousand times." But that is what I wanted to hear—a thousand times, ten thousand times—for it was beautiful and Auntie Rachel was my grandmother's sister and the only member of that generation I could ever meet.

The weather had kept me away from Perth, though perhaps it need not have, for the sun always shone there from a cloudless sky and the winds blew gently and it was always warm. You could slowly climb Kinnoull or saunter peacefully across the North Inch—or you could pull your rowboat softly up the Tay, in your shirt-sleeves, just any day at all. Or so it was in my father's and mother's day. Since I was not entirely confident that this was still so, I did not visit Perth while it was cold and blowy in Edinburgh. But by mid-May the weather was so warm that I fell asleep on the bus somewhere past Stirling and failed to awaken till the Lindsays' street was a mile or two behind me. But it was a pleasant experience—to discover that I was suddenly and magically in Perth, and that it did not matter that I had missed the street. This, after all, was my home and I could find the Lindsays' street as easily as I could find Fourteenth Avenue or Douglas Road.

The Lindsays understood that there were certain things I had to do alone. On the several visits I made there, they would make preliminary arrangements and I could wander off whenever I wished. A visitor usually starts with cemeteries. They are histories for the living. As she searched for the location of the Murdoch stone, the clerk at Wellshill recalled my mother singing in Perth during the first war. It was a simple granite slab, as clean and fresh as when my grandmother was laid there, a few months before my mother sailed for Canada. If she had lived just three or four years more, she could have been cured of the pernicious anaemia that killed her. She would be eighty-six years of age now—and perhaps I would have met her. Helen, the wife of Harry Murdoch.

The Murdoch stone was simple, the same as its neighbours, but far down by the road I could see the slender marble column where my great-grandfather John and most of his fourteen children were buried. I sat on the low cement curb beneath the morning sun and read it in peace. Uncle John was here last September, swathed in his great Mackintosh and his black Homburg, puffing on his pipe and muttering endless incantations. "Grandfather was the first," he said, "in 1880. And Uncle David was the last, in 1937. I mind Aunt Nell. She was an awfie drinker but she was a kind soul. I mind o' the time she said we could keep all the eggs we could find in the barn, but when we got them home we discovered they were a' rotten."

Uncle John is back in Edinburgh now and my great-grandfather's bones have been lying here since 1880. The stone does not tell me where or when he was born. Even Maymie Lindsay, whose mother's name, Christian, is etched here in granite, does not know, though she can tell me more than my father. But am I to languish for the remainder of my life knowing only that a man named John Morton, my great-grandfather, died in 1880 after siring fourteen children? He, too, had a father and a grandfather and a great-grandfather. There must be some record of his origins, and if there is, I will find it. In the meantime I sat beneath the warm sun and gazed upon this stone in wonder. It is old John's legacy to me, along with the names of his fourteen children, amongst which is James, the sixth son, who died at the age of forty years on the first day of December 1891.

If I had roots, they were there in Wellshill—and out the Dunkeld Road at the Muirton. David Lindsay drove me there early one Sabbath morning. He dropped me where the railroad overpass crossed the road. He leaned over to me as I left and said, "Tell your father you were at the Bogle Brig—but it's no' there now." The Bogle Brig? Why yes, I recall the Bogle Brig, and that "bogle" means "ghost." It was torn down and rebuilt. My father used to tell his children of the ghosties at the bridge that carried the railroad north to Aberdeen. To children, its alleged phantoms and its gloom made it a frightening spot. The new overpass is not frightening, at least not on a cloudy Sabbath morning. You can walk under it and up the dyke along the River Almond, which forms the northern boundary of the Muirton where my family farmed for a hundred years. The farm is not as large as I imagined it in my childhood. Far across the fields you can see the cluster of poplars and the stone house which Uncle David rebuilt because, as the story goes, he thought it vibrated. Perhaps it was the ghosties at the Bogle Brig. And then the barns and byres and off in the distance, over near the North Inch, the little cottage on the South Muirton farm where my father's Uncle John lived with his two sisters. My father said that the land there was good for growing beans and neeps. That biscuit barrel in our house—did it not have this John Morton's name on it? Did it not say, engraved into its silver, that this was a prize for his turnip crop?

Up here on the North Muirton, beneath my very feet, John and later David grew barley and oats and tatties and timothy hay—or so my father told me. And here surely is the site of the great rat slaughter on that blood-drenched autumn day so long ago. Two hundred, Uncle John said, "and nary a rat was found on the Muirton for many a year." Walk along the Almond beneath leaden skies and south along the Tay, and here is Woody Island—and across the river, the Palace of Scone, from which the English stole the Stone of Destiny seven hundred years ago. I am behind the farmhouse—and farther south, behind the cottage—and here is the North Inch, on which Charles Edward Stewart trained his wild Highlanders. In that week two hundred years ago I could not have walked this grassy expanse without being threatened by claymore or broadsword. Where would I be now if Charles had continued on to London? Where would I be now if James, the sixth son, had not died in 1891?

But I must hurry on. There is another nest of memories in the North Church. Sit where Maymie Lindsay says my father sat and look upward at the balcony where, Auntie Rachel told me a thousand times, she dandled the twins, my mother and my uncle, "one on one knee, one on the other." And at the choir where stern old Harry Murdoch stood and sang "Comfort Ye" and "Every Valley" and where my mother and my aunt, older now, sat casting sidelong glances at the young gentlemen of the town. I do not hear the sermon and when it is over, an elderly lady asks me if I am a visitor, and for just a moment emotion swells up within me and I cannot answer. A visitor? Why, if you go to Wellshill and the Muirton and . . . but it does not matter. I answer that my mother and father went to this church fifty years ago, and the nice old lady is not nearly as impressed as she should be. But there are others down at St. Leonard's Church where Maymie has gathered my mother's and father's friends, and again names long forgotten come tumbling back into recollection.

I climb Kinnoull in the afternoon and see the Muirton and its barns and byres and the North Inch and the town and the Tay winding down through checkered fields to Dundee. A visitor? To Perth? I have know it all my life. I have never left, though my father did. What cataclysmic disaster drove him to desert all this? Was it economic necessity, a family quarrel? It was probably neither, though I would feel better if it had been both. I cannot imagine my father leaving only for the sake of adventure. Why did he leave his widowed mother, his brother and his numerous aunts and uncles? "No hungry generations tread thee down." Who said that? Keats I believe, but it does not matter. My father had a boundless energy to satisfy. He deserted the Tay and found a new love on the Fraser. We all find ourselves on a river sooner or later. Mine at the moment is the Tay, and it is very beautiful as it twists placidly down to Dundee where my father learned to be an engineer. Must I return to Burnaby? Name me one thing that is of the slightest interest to me in Burnaby. Gillespie's Field? Mr. Holt's gas station? Mr. Whittaker's cows—Nan, Nola, Nifty and Nelly? Nothing. Not even in New Westminster or Vancouver. There will always be nostalgic memories of Bowen Island and you will never have finer friends than Flo and Isabel and Em or Mrs. Healy and the Gibsons—but this is where my family lived long before Mr. Dickens's days in London, before Keats and Johnson and Boswell and Samuel Pepys. Maybe before Boadicea who still stands in her chariot down by Westminster Bridge. Maybe even before Stonehenge. I suppose I must return because the opportunities are better in the New World. They were, too, in my father's time and Scots still emigrate for the same reason. Opportunity, economic necessity. I despise them, but as I stroll morosely past the gate to Murray's Asylum and past my father's home—my grandfather's home—I know I will be forced to accept both opportunity and economic necessity, and I am desperate to let every ounce of Scotland and England diffuse into my soul for two more months.

I dally in Colinton on the outskirts of Edinburgh on a sunny Sunday morning, and find a path leading into the Pentlands and climb upward through the heather. I ask a shepherd's wife for directions and she tells me it will take forty minutes to reach Silverburn "or longer for the likes o' you that doesn't know the way," but I go my own route. I am startled by the sudden flap of grouse wings or by the frantic flight of a hare from beneath my feet. I can feel the heather dust on my legs as I climb higher, and I know that I am a silhouette on the skyline. I am, at least, if anyone sees me—but there is no one here. There is nothing but grouse and hares and heather and hills—and every time I reach another peak, there is yet another, higher. I want to reach the highest peak and look around the world at everything below me, and finally I do—on Scald Law, I believe, for there is nothing higher. I sit and rest my weary bones beside a patch of snow and eat two cream crackers, which I have spirited away from Miss Grant's dinner table, and suck snow to dampen my parched tongue. Carnethy is just across from me and Glencourse below. I skirt the snow and tumble downward and lie on my stomach to drink from a stream and surely there could not be a more magnificent day. I am sorry I must take the bus from Flotterstone, for it is a modern obscenity after walking in the lonesomeness of the hills—but the glory of the day is still with me as I wash the heather dust from my weary limbs in Miss Grant's boarding house in Manor Place.

But I do not have to leave Edinburgh to enjoy myself. I can sit beside the Water of Leith in Dean Village or slip down St. Leonard's Hill to the Dumbiedykes and think of Mrs. Healy. Why do the Dumbiedykes remind me of Mrs. Healy? She used to talk about the Dumbiedykes and Morningside. I can walk about the base of Salisbury Crags and Arthur's Seat and lean against the wind all the way to Duddingston and back through the saddle where Dunsappie's water is blown into great wet sheets sweeping high to the road. The sheep huddle in the sheltered spots on Arthur's Seat and watch me warily, and I scramble from rock to rock but reach the top again and grasp the cairn and hope I will not be blown off and down into Hunter's Bog where Charles Edward Stewart camped so long

ago. I am just a little frightened as I lie there holding tightly to
the cairn, but I can smell the sea-salt blowing in from the
Forth and it is exhilarating. Even though I am exhausted, I feel
I must climb the soft slope to the edge of the crags—and down
again to dally for a moment before Holyrood Palace. I feel the
urge to write to Mrs. Healy—and a month later she answers, in
a beautiful flowing hand, which I did not expect. She says she
still loves her land, but she has fallen upon dark days and she
knows she will never see it again. But, she says, there is no
reason why my parents cannot.

None of our friends in Burnaby will ever see their land
again. It is sad, for they have talked about it all my life and I
think about them when I am in Perth and the Dumbiedykes
and Morningside and Melrose. One day I walked from
Dryburgh to Abbotsford and back again into Galashiels. I stood
in the ruins of Melrose Abbey and thought of Mrs. Gregory
who, many years ago, sat on our couch looking at the photograph in the Scotsman's Calendar and remarked that she had
been born there, "but no' in the Awbbey!" It is an historic site,
not because of its age or beauty, not because of Robert the
Bruce or Walter Scott, but because Mrs. Gregory sat upon our
couch and announced so beautifully that she was born there.

No one would claim that Glenboig is one of the scenic
wonders of the world, but Mrs. Gibson was born in the town.
One warm Sunday morning I took the bus to Coatbridge and I
asked a young fellow where I could find the road to Glenboig.
He answered, "Aye. Ye take this yin," and then, as an afterthought, "Here! I'll take ye me'sel'." He was on his way to
church but he insisted on walking the five miles with me, right
to the door of Hunters' home where Mrs. Gibson's sister lived.
They were a God-fearing couple. They had just returned from
church—and looked askance at me for wandering about the
country on the Sabbath.

Later that afternoon I went on to Dennistoun to visit Flo's
sister-in-law who had married Duncan McCulloch long before
I was born. It did not matter that I had never seen Duncan nor

his wife, nor that she was not home. I had stood on her verandah and rung the doorbell, and a pretty little child told me that Mrs. McCulloch had gone away on a holiday. It mattered that Flo would be pleased.

With the appearance of warm weather I saw less of Uncle John. If he was hurt by the reduction in my visits, he did not show it. One evening, after an absence of a couple of weeks, he said to me as I entered, "Och! I thought you'd be along tonight. The green needs cutting." I had no idea he had any grass, but, indeed, down below at the back there was a high stone wall surrounding a patch of grass and a large border of shrubs and perennials. I hate to admit it but I was rather annoyed—for two reasons. The first was that there were so many things I wanted to do in Edinburgh during my remaining weeks, and gardening was not very high on the list. The second reason was that I had only two sets of clothes: one for hiking in, the other to work in, visit in and appear in public in. I had always referred to them as "old clothes" and "good clothes," though there were some people, I know, who would have preferred the terms "old" and "better" and still others who would have diplomatically avoided a comparison. To save any argument, let us say that I was wearing my visiting clothes that evening—and the shoes common to both my wardrobes.

Actually I cut the grass without soiling my clothes—but then Uncle John decided he wanted the edges trimmed, following which he suggested I weed the border. It was selfish of me, I know, but I became more and more annoyed. He did nothing, though he tried to look busy in his neat, dark suit and maroon bow tie. He just plowtered around, as my father would have said. And he talked and talked. Always talking.

"Do you know what flower this is?" he asked.

"That's rudbeckia, Uncle John."

"Do you know that one over there?"

"Foxglove," I answered, trying valiantly to keep my knees off the damp soil, as my legs and back began to ache.

"Digitalis," he announced triumphantly, and proceeded to

present a long dissertation on the medical uses of the leaf, all the way from darkest Africa to his beloved Royal Infirmary—where, as it happened, I was slaving at the time.

"Do you know what this is?" he asked, following his digitalis oration.

"Cheiranthus," I muttered, hoping to parry any further scientific comment.

"We call it wallflower here."

I had the feeling the old dog was playing with me, making me suffer for ignoring him so long.

"My father used to grow it at Gannochyfold in your mother's garden," I said to him rather coldly.

"Did he tell you that? He's still quite a gardener, is he? I mind o' the time my grandfather's aorta burst . . ."

How could I be angry? I loved his tales, even those he repeated. And I have often thought that I could have done more for him.

On another evening we went to a rugby match east of the city. There was nothing very remarkable about the event except that it was pleasant to be with my uncle. The venture was perhaps of some note in that it was the longest streetcar ride I ever had with Uncle John, and I had had quite a few. To begin with, it is necessary to understand that in Edinburgh car fares increase every six blocks or so by a sum which I never quite remembered, but perhaps it was a ha'penny. Uncle John knew exactly at what street the fares increased and he consequently always got off the streetcar a block before the fares changed, preferring to walk perhaps four or five blocks rather than pay an extra ha'penny and not get his six blocks' worth. The other interesting thing about streetcar riding with Uncle John was that he always sat on the aisle seat on the left side of the car so he could stretch out his right leg to its fullest. His cane was set between his legs, his hands on top of it, and his eyes were always peering straight ahead. You would swear he was oblivious to everything about him and that either he was deeply immersed in his own thoughts or his mind was a complete blank. He never spoke a word, but once off the streetcar he would amaze you with all sorts of detailed observations he had stored away in his mind during the trip.

"Did you see the hands o' yon woman in front o' us?" he asked after we had descended from the car that evening. "She must be an auld fish wifie from Leith."

"There was a wee girl up ahead with an awfie birthmark on her head. Can they do anything about that nowadays?"

"Yon sergeant across the aisle was in the K.O.S.B.s, Fourteenth Army in India. He had the D.C.M. and the Burma Star."

Without any apparent turn of his head, he had been able to read and interpret the ribbons on the soldier's chest. Uncle John was truly remarkable in this regard. To look at him sitting there stolidly, you would never dream that he had noticed a thing.

On the return trip from the rugby match, he insisted on getting off the car at the east end of Princes Street. I do not believe that this was an attempt to deprive the Edinburgh tramway system of a penny or two, though Uncle John was not at all averse to such an act; he was just not yet ready to go home. We walked slowly along the pavement, stopping frequently while he muttered some observations on the goods in the shop windows. "That's Hunting Robertson tartan there. Do you ever see the kilt in Canada? Yon Victor Mature's not the type to be in a biblical picture. He's better in a gangster film. It's awfie bad taste to show women's underwear in the window like that. By Joves, it'll be out o' there by the time the General Assembly meets."

Our progress was extremely slow, but we finally reached the West End about 9:30. From there, Uncle John would catch the car up to Comiston Road while I would go a few blocks west to Manor Place. But he still was not prepared to part. I stood there in front of Binns' shivering in the damp May air—shivering, and listening to Uncle John ramble on. If I had been warm, I would not have minded, but I was cold—and just a little bit angry. I should not have been. Uncle John's only pastimes were to bowl once a week, eat at Binns' daily and chat the hours away in between. At 11:00 I finally told him I had to get to bed, and I ran the whole way home, wondering if this damp chill contributed to my parents' departure from Scotland.

The last of my outings with Uncle John was a visit to the Border country to visit two old friends of my father. When we were children, he told us many tales of his childhood adventures, virtually all of them farm tales, of slaughtering rats or snaring hares—and often, by mistake, the occasional farm cat who happened to use the same route as the hares—or ferreting or guddling for trout, and so many others. We always assumed these took place at the Muirton, though the site did not matter; it was the adventure itself and the people involved that remained so vividly in our memories. Two of the youngsters who played a prominent part in those tales were Tom and Jim Lawrie. I had always considered them legendary figures or possibly the figment of my father's imagination or, at the best, two old fellows who had died a very long time ago. The first time Uncle John mentioned them, I paid little attention, but when he later said he had written to them and that we were going to visit them, I felt like saying, "Come on now, Uncle John, there really aren't two old guys named Tom and Jim Lawrie, are there?" Being just about as canny as my uncle now, I avoided saying so aloud and it is just as well I did, for Tom and Jim Lawrie were indeed alive and well and living in Lauder, down near the Esperson Farm where my father used to visit and where some of his adventures took place.

We set off by bus one misty Saturday afternoon in June, through the rolling countryside to the little village near the border—and there they were, as large as life, sitting comfortably in a small stone cottage. Tom was a compact fellow with sharp features and the weathered face of a farmer. Jim was just the opposite. He was a huge fellow in both height and girth, with rounder features—and it was Jim Lawrie who was the best shot Uncle John had ever seen. It was he who had "shot the hare right oot the dug's mouth."

Three old men talking—two childhood friends of my father and my father's brother—talking endlessly of events that perhaps they had never before recollected. Do you mind old Geordie, the horse that came back from the Boer War, John? Aye. And I mind the straw enclosures we put up for lambing, Tom, and how we'd cut the lambs' tails at six weeks of age. Aye. And if their mother died we'd feed them by the bottle—a quart of milk three times a day. And do you mind guddling for trout in the brook? And cinching? Your father was the best cincher in the country. He could slip a wire loop over a trout's head and whip it up to the bank better than anyone I ever knew. And sometimes we'd drop lime shells from the lime kiln into the deepest holes we couldn't get at and the lime would take all the oxygen out of the water and the trout would rise, gasping for air, and we'd scoop them out.

Tom was concerned that their tales would bore me. They did not. I had heard most of them from my father's lips when I was a child, many of which I recollected only when they were repeated. But that was five thousand miles away and I was a child and I had heard tales of King Arthur and his Knights of the Round Table and they had all seemed to be mere fairy tales. But these stories were true—and they happened right here, within a mile of where I was sitting.

After tea Uncle John, Tom and I walked slowly about the farm and again it was fascinating to hear them talk to each other. On such occasions Scottish people will break into a distinctive dialect. This happened in Blairgowrie when David Lindsay spoke to his workmen in the huge barn where he stored potatoes. I could understand David perfectly when he spoke directly to me, but I did not understand a word of the

conversation he had with his workmen. It was not quite the
same with Uncle John and Tom Lawrie, but they used strange
terms and they spoke in short, abrupt sentences in a detatched,
almost absent-minded manner. Tom wore a rough tweed suit,
the bottom of his trousers clasping the tops of his dress boots. A
deerstalker hat drooped over his ears. Uncle John wore his
usual dark suit, white shirt, maroon bow tie and black Homburg. A real city slicker.

"Yon post needs replacin', Tom."

"It'll do a wee while yet, John."

"Y'r tatties is awfie early, Tom."

"Aye."

"Yon Bishop's Weed is gettin' ahead o' ye, Tom."

"It'll be a' oot next back end, John."

"Ye mind how we used to guddle at Esperson, Tom?"

"Aye. I was the best guddler there was. Still am."

"Y'r dykes is holdin' fine, Tom."

"Been there a hundred years, John. Two hundred more t'
go."

"Ye mind the neeps we used to eat raw, Tom?"

"Aye. Swedes they were."

"My Uncle David used to eat them with his pocket knife,
right oot the ground."

"A ferret once put his teeth right through y'r father's hand,
right up there on the hill," Tom said to me.

I wanted to answer, "Aye. I mind o' the time," but I said
only, "Yes, my father has told me."

Tom remembered so many of my father's childhood tales.
He was also quite concerned that I would not understand the
words he and Uncle John used. I indeed did not know that
"the back end" was autumn, but how could I possibly spend
my childhood with my father and not know the meaning of
"tatties" and "neeps" and "guddle"? How could I possibly not
know a dry-stane dyke—especially since they seemed to criss-
cross Scotland in every direction, rising steeply and neatly up
hills and dropping down into valleys, as if they had been

drawn on a piece of grey-blue linen tracing paper by my father's finest pen?

Uncle John had no desire to leave. He looked quite startled when Tom informed us that the last bus for Edinburgh departed at 8:20 P.M. He was prepared to gossip on till midnight, but there was no choice. We thanked the Lawries for a pleasant day, Tom replied in his usual manner, "Nae bother at a'," we clambered aboard the bus and I immediately began to compose a letter to my father, telling him that I had actually seen and talked to Tom and Jim Lawrie.

And so up that beautiful, rolling countryside, the hills still bathed in mist and the fields—crisscrossed by the ever-present dry-stane dykes—the freshest shade of green that ever one could see. But Uncle John was in no hurry to get home. He insisted on leaving the bus at the east end of Princes Street and limping all the way to Lothian Road, with stops at almost every shop window. He rarely said a word on the bus, but poking laboriously along Princes Street he kept up a constant monologue on any subject that happened to stimulate his mind, the words drawling slowly but steadily as he plodded on, with the occasional stop to catch his breath. "I mind you used to be able to buy a pair o' socks for one an' six but now you canna buy them for less than four shillin's. They'll be startin' the dances below the castle before long. I've never danced but a few times in my life. Did you know the Forth Bridge is two and a half inches longer in the summer than in the winter? It's a cantilever bridge. Your father would know all about that. I see Harry Gordon is comin' to town. He's an awfie one for makin' jokes about the General Assembly."

Outside Binns' he hung his cane on his arm, lit up his pipe, sank his hands into his Mackintosh and prepared himself for a good blether. This time I did not mind. It was warmer now and I knew I had little time remaining to spend with my uncle. We talked until he could no longer suck smoke from his pipe and we parted for Comiston Road and Manor Place.

It was almost over now. I knew I did not want to return to

the New World just as perhaps my father did not want to leave the Old. But I was going. Unwillingly. There were desperate last visits to Kirkcudbright and the Lindsays and Auntie Rachel before I took the bus to Perth. On this occasion I was merely passing through.

I walk up South Methven and North Methven and up Balhousie Street and stop a moment at Number 63—Dunearn—where my mother was born. But I cannot dally now. Around the corner to the north is old John's cottage and the football field they call Muirton Park—and then the Dunkeld Road. I step slowly past the Toll House and past the cluster of farm buildings where my great-grandfather lived over a hundred years ago. The clouds gather now, there is a flash of lightning, a clap of thunder and the rain pours down. Is someone displeased with me for leaving? I run for shelter. As the rain slants down, I realize that I am standing beneath the Bogle Brig—though it's no' there now. It is a fitting place to be in a thunderstorm. But the rain soon stops, I turn to the north, look back once as I cross the Almond and tell myself, as my mother and father did thirty years ago, that I will soon return. But I turn once more, and yet again, for a last look at the Muirton—until the road bends and I am left only with a deep, searing sorrow, and I realize that I am a fool for being so sentimental. All those old Johns and Williams and Andrews would never allow a tear to hang precariously upon their eyelids, though my mother would.

Walk and hitchhike—except in the Western Highlands on the Sabbath where, I am told, Sunday Observance must be respected. Here is Birnam, which Shakespeare mentions. What was that Englishman doing up here? Surely he never came, for Dunsinane is a very long distance away. And Pitlochry. To the villagers, it is famous for its dam and its theatre—they play *Macbeth* tomorrow—but to me it is the home of Mr. Donald Stewart. And the Tummel and the Garry and the Pass of Killiecrankie, and I climb a great rock at the Soldier's Leap—

which I have seen in the Scotsman's Calendar. I walk in the rain and sunshine and ride in Rolls Royces, Rovers, delivery vans, lorries and motorcycles all the way to Inverness and Carbisdale and the Kyles of Bute and Thurso—but I must pay to cross in the ferry to the Orkneys.

It is a desolate country. Beautiful but desolate. Mr. Dickens would not like it. He is a city type. He loves the man-swarm. The Orkneys would be an abomination to him. He would take no interest in Standing Stones or stone circles at Brogard or Maes Howe or runic inscriptions. He would find no fascination in watching shepherds shear their sheep in Glen Nevis—talking to each other in a strange tongue. It is the tongue I heard long ago on the Christmas evening when Mrs. MacLeod sat on our couch and spoke in Gaelic to Mi-cah. Mr. Dickens would not be amused to see the new-shorn sheep leap high in the air with the weight of their winter coat lifted from their shoulders, nor would he be interested to hear the shout of "Beast!" when the shepherd is ready for the next. He would rather be on Doughty Street than leaning on a fence listening to a shepherd call to his dog, high on the hills as he guides his sheep. Hear him? "In back; in back," he calls, then, "Come to me; come to me." The dog is happy. He races. Absolutely races—and stops momentarily at a stream for two licks of water—and races on again. "Come to me; come to me." He is a happy dog.

But Mr. Dickens would not be interested. He would be fascinated, however, in the Youth Hostel in Glencoe—at least if he had managed to keep dry that day. He would love the stench of blocked water closets and of wet clothes, wet socks, wet bodies, and a variety of foods cooking on wet stoves. He would love the swarm of half-naked bodies, some shoeless, some in socks, some in great muddy boots, bustling about on the wet, muddy floor. And the clamour of a thousand coarse voices—of men and women, old and young, fat and slim, shaven and unshaven. Mr. Dickens would be fascinated by wet walkers and bicyclers from Edinburgh and Glasgow in the first week of July: he would be fascinated for a few moments, he would store the scenes and smells in his mind, and then he would flee the dreadful nightmare and retreat to Doughty Street, where there is warmth and cleanliness and dryness and comfort.

I leave the nightmare behind me as early as I can the next morning and wash and shave in a mountain stream—and wander peacefully through the Western Highlands. I am dreadfully hungry, as I always seem to be, but I am happy now. This is Isabel's country. She painted it—and I remember she once proudly announced that she was not Scottish, she was Hieland. And this is Oban, tucked behind the hills beside the ocean. I feel strangely at home because Mi-cah and Flo and Isabel were born here and talked about it all my life. Mr. Munro is working on his dock. Flo said he would be there. How did she know? She has not been here for fifty years—but he probably did the same thing then. And he remembers them. Perhaps he had an eye for Isabel once. She must have been beautiful in her youth. They are all too reserved to admit to such affairs, however; in fact, Mr. Munro accepts my visit rather calmly. How could anyone leave this lovely village on the Firth of Lorne? How could anyone choose Burnaby over Oban? Perhaps they were sorry they left. Certainly they speak proudly and nostalgically of the town—and they named their home Lorne Villa. You could see it printed in the cement as you walked up the front path between the rowan and cherry trees, and from the balcony the letters were very small and upside down.

There is little time now. Can I afford a day—and twenty-five shillings—to sail around the Western Islands on one of Mr. MacBrayne's old steamers? If Samuel Johnson can do it, so must I. But I cannot expect to eat, too. I lean on the rail and see Isabel's paintings spread before me. There are great steep ridges plunging into the sea, and others—and others behind them: green, then blue, then grey paling into white. Poor Isabel. She will never see these hills again.

I am a trifle uncomfortable on the steamer, for I am more than a mere passenger—I am a tourist. Indeed, I am more than a tourist. I am a dirty, ragged tourist who has not had a bath for almost two weeks—and does not care. No one else seems to care either. I lean on the rail as we slide into Tobermory Bay. There is a dock crowded with people and I feel I am sliding into Snug Cove on the *Lady Alexandra.* In fact, Mr. Mac-Brayne's old steamer is an exact replica of the "*Alex.*" Remember that miserable Scotch terrier at Mount Gardner? He was named Toby after this very town on the Island of Mull.

Now you can see Skye and Eigg and Rumm and South Uist. Is that not where Charles Edward Stewart landed before he marched on to Glenfillan and the North Inch? And Eriskay. My mother used to sing "The Eriskay Love Lilt." And now I risk my life stepping aboard a rolling motor launch to enter Fingal's Cave on Staffa. Surely Mendelssohn did not imperil his future by such a foolhardy act. They did not have motors then. Nor gramophone records. I chance my life again at Iona, as St. Columba did, and do not wish to leave; but the train will be waiting for me at Waverley in just three more days and I must keep moving. I can only drink in the sights and sounds of past and present. It is not until I am within the harbour of Oban again that I realize I am weak with hunger—and a kind old lady gives me two glucose tablets to help me on to Dalmally.

At Crianlarich I am back in Perthshire again and wander slowly into the Trossach's wildest nook. Mr. Fennel pounded "The Lady of the Lake" into my young head at Edmonds Street School many years ago. "The stag at eve had drunk his fill, / Where danced the moon on Monan's Rill, / And deep his midnight lair had made / In lone Glenartney's hazel shade"; I still remember it. And it is all here. The Brig o' Turk, Ellen's Isle, Ben Venue, Ben Voirlich. I sit beside Loch Achray and my heart weeps. I have been here before. Last fall I took the bus to Aberfoyle and walked across Duke's Pass to this very spot. I look back once more, and a tear of pleasure and sorrow hangs heavily in my heart—and I climb slowly upward, neither hearing nor seeing. And suddenly, when I am completely alone near the top of the pass, I hear a lady's voice say, "Would you prefer to walk or would you like a ride?" I had not noticed her. She speaks from a car at the side of the road. She passed me twice this morning, she says, but she did not offer me a ride because I seemed engrossed. I accept, for I know that it is over now.

I sleep at Loch Ard, and the next afternoon I stretch out on the grass beneath the castle. I am tired and ragged and dusty, and Uncle John is expecting me—but I do not want to see Uncle John nor Montreal nor Burnaby. I want to lie here forever on the grass, and visit Perth and Orkney and Oban and Iona. Instead I trudge painfully down to Manor Place, I bare my soul to Miss Grant and her "heart is fu'." Have a bath, stay the night as her guest and you will feel better in the morning, she says. And she is correct.

"Come away in," Uncle John said to me the next day, as if I had never been away. He was reasonably interested in my trip, though almost every little incident I recounted to him minded him o' the time . . . and he would ramble away about recollections of other days. He had no desire to go to the Empire Theatre to see *Don Juan in Hell*—and perhaps it was a strange way to spend my second to last evening in Edinburgh. My thoughts were far from hell, and it was very noisy in the gallery. "That fairly gets your teeth on edge," Uncle John remarked when I told him. It was one of his favourite expressions.

I slept in the kitchen that night and did not even allow myself a glance at the shelf on which he stored his oat cakes. But in the morning there was porridge and treacle and tea, after which I had several errands to complete. But there was really no necessity* to drift down the Canongate to the park and to Arthur's Seat. I should have stayed with Uncle John— but I was still desperate. I climbed the Seat for the last time and felt the fresh sea-salt blow in from Inchkeith, and I strolled slowly up the slope of Salisbury Crags and looked down upon the chimneys of Edinburgh. I knew it was over now. But remember old Boswell? When he left Edinburgh for London, he stood at the foot of the Canongate and bowed thrice to Arthur's Seat and thrice to St. Anthony's Chapel above St. Margaret's Loch. He succumbed to whims. I did too. And I did not forget the Crags. Thrice to Salisbury Crags.

I wrote two letters that afternoon while Uncle John read the newspaper across from me. But he was an inveterate communicator. Everything he came upon, he read to me. My father had the same habit; my mother had no need to read the newspaper after my father had finished reading it to her. And we had a very special tea that afternoon—in the dining room, which was the only time I ever saw Uncle John use it for its chosen purpose. He slowly set the table with plates, knives, sugar, milk and jam, limping back and forth from the kitchen, bringing one article at a time.

"If you'll tell me where the butter is, Uncle John, I'll get it for you," I said, trying to be helpful.

"Och!" he answered. "We'll be puttin' jam on our scones. There's no need for butter."

How many hours can you spend talking to your uncle? Is it possible to sit from 6:00 P.M., with only a short break for news at 9:00, without the conversation lagging, without physical discomfort, without being bored? It is. He slouches low in his chair, his right leg stretched far out upon the carpet, his arms resting on his chair, his pipe ashes falling gently onto his waistcoat as he talks and smokes at the same time. He is so neat and clean and relaxed and contented. It is my last evening with my Uncle John and every word he mutters through his pipe is sweet to me.

During my absence he had collected a number of newspaper clippings which he now read to me ponderously, with frequent editorial comment. When these were exhausted we moved to his favourite subjects—the British Legion, patent medicines,

Highland regiments, and the Royal Agricultural Fair. He then minded o' the time an insolent Scottish bee stung him on his proud Scottish forehead. "But," he announced triumphantly at the end of his tale, "there's one thing—that bee did na' sting anyone else, for I put my foot on him." He then reprimanded me gently for failing to destroy letters I received. At first I could not understand the point he was attempting to make since, at that time, my life was an unblemished one. It seems, however, that while I was touring in the north, he had emptied a wastebasket and had found the letter I had received from Mrs. Healy, which he dutifully tore into little pieces. I could see him doing it—lifting the wastebasket awkwardly, with his stiff leg stretched out, glancing at its contents, noting the intact letter, perhaps muttering to himself, "Hello! What's this?", reading the return address, and being tempted to read the rest—but thinking better of it, and slowly, deliberately tearing it into little pieces so no one could read the secret communication between an elderly lady and a young man. I suspect he was disappointed when I told him the unexciting truth. We then turned to a newspaper clipping I had received, describing my brother's recent wedding. He slowly read the complete item aloud, stopping after almost each sentence to comment or ask a question, drawling through his pipe quietly and sending little showers of ashes floating up and down onto his waistcoat. " 'They will drive down the Oregon coast,' " he muttered, " 'the bride travelling in a powder blue gabardine suit, with matching straw hat and wine accessories.' That's an awfie outfit to be drivin' down the Oregon coast in . . ."

And when I showed him a photograph in my wallet, he did not give the wallet back to me when he had finished. He dug into its secret recesses and poured slowly through the numerous and sundry documents that had collected there, each of which he examined carefully and commented upon in great detail—an old driver's licence, a Youth Hostels Association card, a United States Coast Guard pass, a wartime registration card, an old library card, and many other unimportant documents. Uncle John enjoyed the little things.

I watched him in the morning as he lit the grate and placed a pot of water on to boil. I watched him as he awaited the noisy bubble to stir him slowly into action. I watched him as he reached into his sack of oats and let the precious grain trickle through his stubby fingers, stirring so deliberately and steadily with his worn old wooden stick in his other hand. I watched him reach into the sack again, and again—and the oats dribbled through his fingers. I watched as he lifted the glutinous mass out on his stick in one great glob and I watched as he cut it with a knife into two plates. I watched him pour heavy black treacle over his and I accepted the can as he pushed it over to me. I watched him sip slowly from his magnificent cup—in which my mother could easily have mixed a cake. It was porridge, treacle and tea—and the train.

We said good-bye to each other as we always did, as if I just might be back next week, and I struggled down the winding staircase, called good-bye again to the small, neat figure up on the fourth-floor landing, and departed as I had arrived last September, by the Comiston Road streetcar. It was different now, though. Then I had stood in fear on his doorstep. I crossed it now with regret. Perhaps Uncle John watched me from his window, standing well back so I would not see him. I hope he did. Perhaps he was sad to see me go. I hope he was. But I knew that I would return someday to chat away the evening with my Uncle John. I knew, because thirty years ago my mother and father had known that someday they, too, would return.

As the *Empress of France* plunges across the Irish Sea, I ask myself again, why am I leaving? It is pointless. I have asked the same question a thousand times and the answer is always the same, always exasperatingly practical. There is greater opportunity in the New World. I sit morosely on the deck dreaming, half-asleep. With each plunge of the ship I am slipping farther and farther away and there is no Mr. Dougal to ease the pain. New World voices are offensive. The New World is offensive.

I languish for a year in Montreal before I see Burnaby again, but a year does not blunt my longing to return to Britain. There is a dull ache in my heart—and the empty house on Fourteenth Avenue does nothing to improve my depression. The grass is uncut, the vegetables are growing wildly, the flower plots are in disarray and the driveway is green with weeds. The house, however, is empty for a worthy reason: my mother and father are in Scotland. The millenium has been reached. It is September 1952, thirty-three years since they departed, and I am happy for them, though deeply anguished that I am not there with them.

But there is more than anguish. There is lonesomeness—and the feeling that I no longer belong here. There is only one cure: work. I hack away desperately at the weeds on the driveway to keep my mind from Salisbury Crags and Doughty Street. I hack and hack till I reach the pillars at the foot of the driveway and see the name on the gate my father built. Gannochy. It is more than a year now but I can still see the name on the gate of my father's home—my grandfather's home—in Perth. Gannochyfold. I turn to the hedge that now hides the rustic fence which my father built by the sweat of his brow so many years ago. There are only a few dry cedar posts remaining, weathered and rotten, supported by the hedge surrounding it. But they are there to remind me. Fourteenth Avenue has changed, too. Burnaby has sewers now. There are no damp ditches clogged with weeds and all sorts of horrible things, and I miss them. There are no potholes either. There is a smooth, hard asphalt surface where I used to pull up melted tar to chew, and there are neat cement curbs, so perfect that they look as if they had been squeezed from a giant tube of toothpaste.

Old family friends pass and stop to talk—of their illnesses, of the doctors they have seen, and of the pink medicines they drink and the green pills they swallow. Emerson Doran turns his car into the driveway. There is a great stir of pleasure in my heart. He shakes hands and says that Flo is still depressed over the death of Isabel a year or so ago. But a trace of his old sense of humour shows as he tells funny little stories of the two sisters, and I think how angry Flo would be if she knew. There are occasional "hells" and "damns" in Em's speech, which I do not recall from my childhood—though his raspy laugh is still familiar. He shakes hands again and drives away, and I glow in the pleasure of seeing him again. Yet there is something different. He no longer treats me as a child. He shakes hands and tells me secret stories. He confides in me, and "damn" and "hell" sound strange on his lips. He has treated me as an adult and it is discomfitting.

I visit my brother and his new wife; and my sister, who has a child. I am an uncle? Like Uncle John? I visit the Gibsons on Burgess Street and talk of Glenboig, and the Stuarts who still live their sterile existence on London Street and talk of Pitlochry; and I visit Mrs. Healy on Eighth Avenue and speak of Morningside and the Dumbiedykes and of her letter, about which Uncle John scolded me for not destroying. They talk, too, of illnesses and doctors.

Flo and Em invite me for dinner and I ring the rattling bell at the front door and wander through the great house of a hundred gables, full of so many memories. The door to the balcony is locked, but through the window I can see that the floorboards are warped, the paint is peeling from the balustrades and the flower boxes are decayed. Flo bustles about preparing her dinner, already late, but she speaks little. They take me for a drive to see the changes in Burnaby, and they stop for an ice cream cone, and I suddenly realize that this is what they used to do in my childhood. And yet, when I get up to leave after coffee, Em stands awkwardly and tells me that they very much enjoyed my visit. He says that they were afraid to invite me, afraid that a young fellow would not enjoy the company of the old. He shakes hands with me and I return to the empty house with a strange mixture of pleasure and sorrow.

My mother and father returned on the sixth day of September, full of the pleasures of their journey. We talked for hours and our home lived again. We sat, too, looking endlessly at colour slides my father had taken. A year or so previously he had adapted an ancient magic lantern to project 35-mm slides but, alas, after his patient work, he had been presented with a fine modern projector on his retirement. His adaptation of the old, he said, was every bit as good as its modern equivalent—and he was quite correct, though it was hardly as compact.

And he set out to complete one of his last projects: a detailed record of the memorable trip to Scotland. He had stored away every ticket stub, map, menu, telegram, newspaper clipping, brochure, guide, program—every single memento he could lay his hands on. He drew up a detailed itinerary of the 2,291 miles he drove in the Wyvern Vauxhall he had rented, every village he passed through, the mileage, the time, the hotels, the people he met, the cost—everything. And, so typical of everything he did, he pasted them into the strongest loose-leaf book he could find. It was not up to his usual standard of practicality, like the *Samson* bed or the desk or the chest of drawers, but he set out to do it with his usual patience and enthusiasm, and when he completed it, he could sit back and say he had done a thorough job. It was neither maudlin nor sentimental. It was merely the record of a great event which he felt impelled to complete, for reasons known only to himself.

My mother knew how much I longed to return to Britain. As we sat talking on the evening before I departed again for Montreal, she stated clearly and innocently that we would go together next time. Perhaps she knew she would not, though she could not admit it. My father remained silent.

six

There was a sign on a grey stone building on North St. David Street in Edinburgh which read, "Scottish Ancestry Research Society." In 1951, after passing it on several occasions, I entered to find a bare room with a table at one end, behind which sat a middle-aged man and woman, presumably awaiting the appearance of a ragged colonial. This one could not afford ten pounds. By late 1953, however, I was slightly more solvent and just as curious. The little room on North St. David Street activated itself and I patiently awaited the appearance of my pedigree. Would I be the descendant of the Duc de Mortaigne who sailed with William in 1066? More likely, I sprang from a town on the edge of a moor—or muir. Mere peasant stock.

The reply came the following April in a series of brief and impersonal, but succinct, statements, many of them at least interestingly worded. "Prior to 1855," the introduction read, "registration of births and marriages in Scotland were voluntarily recorded in the old parish registers (unindexed) of each parish." They had found a name in a Perth parochial register:

> James Morton lawful son to John Morton, Farmer, in said Parish and Helen Bowes his spouse, baptised 26th May 1850 by the Revd. David Young Minister of the North United Presbyterian Church.

Mere statement of cold fact—but this is James, the sixth son, my grandfather, whom even my father did not know. There were the names of other sons and daughters in that register, but there was no record of the birth of John, the father. The census figures of 1861, however, mentioned that he was born in Forgandenny and the search shifted five miles or so to the south. There followed more lists of marriages and births until yet another John Morton was found to have married in 1755. The parish registers of Forgandenny and several surrounding parishes were then searched back to 1715, but no record of John was found. "The investigation was therefore concluded," the document announced to me sadly.

As the researchers later showed, the male members of my family have always been somewhat retarded in their amorous pursuits. All were married between the ages of thirty-two and thirty-five years through five generations. Surely this early John would not have been more than forty years of age when he married in 1755. The year 1715, then, was a reasonable time at which to close the books on John. Perhaps he was born in a more distant parish or perhaps his parents had more important matters on their minds than the mere registration of a son's birth. Scotland was in the midst of a tumultuous period in its history. After the last of the Catholic Stewart kings, James II (James VII by Scottish reckoning), had been deposed and exiled to France in 1688, William and Mary, then Anne had come to the throne. Since none of these had surviving children, the authorities turned to the distant relatives of the Stewarts in Hanover, and the Protestant George I ascended the throne. By this time, the son of James II had grown to manhood in France. He attempted to regain the throne for the ancient Scottish House of Stewart by armed rebellion in Scotland in 1715. He was known as the Old Pretender—the White Cockade was his emblem—and he was easily defeated.

Over the next thirty years, during which John Morton must have been born, there were constant rumours of secret agents and further revolutions in Scotland, and in 1745, when John of

Forgandenny was surely in his twenties, the son of the Old Pretender, Charles Edward Stewart—also known as the Young Pretender or Bonnie Prince Charlie—slipped into Scotland from France, called the Highlanders to arms, trained them on the North Inch and marched southward towards London. It was at this point—or so I like to think—that John Morton glanced up from his field of neeps on the Gallowmuir Farm to behold the Young Pretender and his band of Highlanders marching down the dusty road from Perth, just as possibly his father beheld the White Cockade of the Old Pretender marching down the same dusty road thirty years earlier. Young Charles almost reached the gates of London, but he was driven back to Culloden where, alas, he was defeated in 1746 by the bloodthirsty Duke of Cumberland and his English troops.

The place and date of John's birth are not known, but the year of his marriage is faithfully recorded in the Forgandenny register:

> May 15th John Morton in this parish and Christian Miller in the parish of Aberdalgie gave up their names for proclamation, in order to marriage, and upon sufficient Testimonial in favours of said Christian they were proclaimed the three subsequent Sabbaths and were married on 18th June 1755.

Christian? Why, that is the name of Maymie Lindsay's mother, still carved in stone in Wellshill, and, though I did not foresee it in 1954, it would be the name of my daughter.

And 1755? We all have our own capricious interests. I am not, for instance, particularly intrigued by the knowledge that the leading politician of the day was William Pitt, but I am fascinated to consider that, as John and Christian were being united, George Frederick Handel was living out his last days in London. Had they ever heard of him on the distant fields of Gallowmuir? They could not have heard of Mozart since he was born the year after the marriage—but Haydn? Probably not, for that very year was the turning point in his professional

career. A humble farmer howking his neeps in the wilds of the
north would also be unaware that two young men from
Lichfield, Samuel Johnson and David Garrick, were now the
leading lights in London's literary and dramatic circles. Indeed,
Johnson published his monumental dictionary in the very year
of John and Christian's marriage. They almost certainly did
not know that they were living in the golden years of art and
literature in England—and certainly they were unaware that a
fifteen-year-old Scot, James Boswell, was studying in Edinburgh just a few miles to the south. It is also fascinating to
realize that in the year of their marriage not a single white man
had gazed upon the rocky coast that is now my home. John
and Christian probably knew very little of the world about
them, though they would have been aware that, in the cruel
wake of Culloden, the kilt and the bagpipe were forbidden in
Scotland and that hundreds of persecuted Highlanders were
emigrating to the eastern extremities of the New World.

Between 1762 and 1775 John and Christian had eight children, including two sets of twins, all born in Forgandenny. The
seventh child, Andrew, was born in 1772, the year before
Boswell and Johnson visited Sir Alexander Gordon in Aber-
brothock (now Arbroath) on their journey to the Western
Islands of Scotland. At the age of sixteen Andrew was working
for his father, now tenant of the Gallowmuir, when Charles
Edward Stewart died in 1788—forgotten—in Rome. And at the
ripe old age of thirty-four years Andrew married Elisabeth
Thomson, "daughter to John Thomson, Tenant in Easter Gos-
pitry in the Parish of Strathmiglo." This couple added seven
children to the family tree. Their first, the third John since
1755, was born in Forgandenny in 1808 at which time his
father was tenant of the Gallowmuir. The head of the family
in two succeeding generations, then, was not a humble plough-
man but the farm manager for the Crown vassal.

The third John was baptized at the age of seven days on "the
29th curt. in his father's house by an ante burgher minister."

He missed Trafalgar but would be seven years of age when Wellington fought at Waterloo. Robert Burns had died a few years earlier, but a new matinee idol, Walter Scott, had taken his place and was happily building his dream house at Abbotsford. About the same time, Thomas Carlyle, at the age of thirteen, walked the eighty-odd miles from his home in Ecclefechan to Edinburgh to further his education.

This was the world into which the third John Morton was born, though his personal world was undoubtedly confined to the few miles surrounding the Gallowmuir. He must have been brought up there since his six brothers and sisters were born there, the last in 1820 when his father, Andrew, was forty-eight years of age. But John moved from the farm, on which his family had toiled for almost a century, just as his aunts and uncles had moved at earlier dates to form new branches of the Morton tree. The date of his departure and the reason for it are not known. He was the eldest son and could presumably have occupied the tenancy of the Gallowmuir on the death of his father. Perhaps the lease had run its course, or perhaps John, like so many of his future sons, merely wished to travel and see the world—or perhaps he wished to be closer to Helen Bowes, the daughter of a Perth labourer. We only know that he married Helen in the Kinnoull Street Church, Perth, on 8 June 1842.

Perhaps he arrived a year or so before that date. In the register he is listed as "farmer servant at the Muirtown in the East Parish of Perth," suggesting that he was not the tenant. The statement also suggests the original name of the farm, unless it was a spelling mistake, an occurrence not uncommon in the registers. It is not known when this third John became the tenant farmer for the Crown vassal, the Earl of Mansfield. The census of 1861 states that he is the head of the family, that he farms 307 acres of the North Muirton and employs eight men, two boys and ten women. He was fifty-two at this time, his wife forty-four. The census also lists ten children. One had died in infancy, two more had yet to be born and one had presumably left home. These were the fourteen children whose names were carved in stone, together with those of their mother and father, in Wellshill. This is where the path into the past had begun, then dwindled into oblivion with the marriage of the first John and Christian Miller in 1755.

But there were new paths now. With the help of my father and Maymie Lindsay, the lives of the fourteen children could be traced in considerable detail, though not all had played an important part in the life of my father. He became partially dependent upon some uncles and aunts while others were merely casual relatives and still others became legends. Andrew, the first-born, was one of the latter, as mysterious and enigmatic an uncle as anyone could have. He must have left home by 1861, almost thirty years before my father was born. He can be traced to Glasgow, Australia and China, where he established Morton's Bank in Shanghai and became a wealthy man. But then he reappears in New Mexico as a rancher and finally as a banker in California, where he accumulated another great fortune. To my father as a child, Uncle Andrew must have been the ideal example of the ambitious young Scot who escapes from home, travels to the most exotic corners of the world and gains great wealth. There are tales, however, suggesting that Andrew was the skeleton in the family closet. My father, when confronted with the information disclosed by the 1861 census, was most surprised to see that Andrew, the eldest son, had left home before the age of eighteen years. And had he lived long enough to read old John's will, my father would have been even more startled. In 1880, at the age of seventy-three, the patriarch of the family died, leaving a will which was read, filed away and forgotten until the original was dusted off in an Edinburgh registry in the early 1960s. It is written in a beautiful copperplate hand and signed clearly and firmly by old John himself in 1875. In the third clause, referring to the disposal of the farm, he declared "that if my eldest son Andrew should interfere with their [his trustees] doing so, he shall thereby forfeit all interest in my means and Estates." The list of executors includes "my sons John, James and George Morton." The witnesses and executors signed the document—and there before my eyes is the signature of my grandfather, "Jas. Morton." He was thirty years of age; he would be married in one year and be dead in eleven.

No one now knows the reason for Andrew's apparent disgrace. He remains a romantic, if not enigmatic, figure and was perhaps the most successful of the children, if wealth is the criterion for success. He died in California in 1919 at the age of seventy-six.

My father often spoke to us of John, the second son—and fourth of this name in four generations—born in 1844. He became tenant of the Muirton when his father died in 1880.

William, the third son, became a legend. It was he who was bitten by a snake in Peru where he died in 1890 when my father was two years of age. The fifth and seventh sons, in a sense, too, were legends. Henry and Robert Morton emigrated to Canada in 1877, three years before their father's death and six years before the railroad crossed the country. Both created farms from the wilderness in Elphinstone, Manitoba, where their families, greatly increased, still live.

George and Thomas were casual relatives living in Dundee and Glasgow, but David, the ninth son and twelfth child of John and Helen Morton, became an important figure in my father's life. To me he is not merely a name carved in stone in Wellshill. He died when I was fifteen, yet I knew him well. My father spoke of him, wrote of him, kept mementoes of him, preserved photographs of him and filed away in his papers the newspaper clipping announcing his death in 1937 at the age of seventy-six.

There was little future for David at the Muirton with John, seventeen years his senior, holding the tenancy. In 1887 he sailed off to New Zealand to become a sheep farmer. He remained there for eleven years and returned in 1898, carrying with him a heavy white turtle-neck sweater which he presented to the son of his brother James, who had died in 1890. My father, ten years of age at the time, had never before seen his uncle. He wore that sweater as he pressed his spade deeply into the damp spring earth on Fourteenth Avenue, as he gently pulled Alf Wells's old clinker-built rowboat at Bowen Island and as he baited his children's fish hooks with salmon roe on the beach at the mouth of the Fraser. It is no longer as white as it must once have been and certainly it is more tattered, but it is still my father's sweater, my great-uncle's sweater, long outliving its owners. It may even outlive me.

David became tenant of the North Muirton and John moved to a small stone cottage on the South Muirton. The reason for the change is not clear. John was a great stout bachelor of two hundred pounds at the age of fifty-four years. Perhaps he was ill or perhaps he merely preferred the quieter life on the South Muirton with his two spinster sisters, Elizabeth and Chattie. David was thirty-seven years of age when he returned from new Zealand. He must have been at least thirty-eight when he married Helen Miller (my father's Aunt Nell), carrying on the strange family tradition of marrying rather late in life. For more than six generations this has resulted in Morton children never having had the opportunity to meet their paternal grandfather—or if they have, it has been only briefly and at a very young age. Paternal grandmothers, often being much younger, have been more available. David had one child, a daughter, whose grandfather had died twenty years earlier and whose grandmother had died seven years before her birth.

And what manner of man was this David who was the only male adult to have any influence on my father during his youth? My old Uncle John (the fifth of that name) sat stolidly in his chair on Comiston Road and muttered through his pipe, "He was a mean devil, was Uncle David," referring presumably to his Scottish frugality, a trait best exemplified by my

Uncle John himself. My father did not entirely deny this. In answer to my written questions, he pressed his pencil deeply into his little pad of pink paper. "The financial aid from the Muirton was minor," he wrote, "—a flagon of milk every week, perhaps a dozen eggs, too, maybe sixpence to we boys, a chicken once in a while, two loads of dung (cow and horse) for the garden from a city byre (stable) as all manure on the farm had to be put back on the land." My father went on to say that he won a ten-pound bursary which allowed him to attend Perth Academy for two years. For the remaining two years he would go to his Uncle David and be given the fee for the next quarter.

The Muirton apparently flourished under David's management. He seems to have lived the life of the gentleman farmer in spite of his alleged frugality, or perhaps because of it. He installed a croquet lawn in the garden—probably the origin of my father's interest in the game. He appears in photographs with his wife, dressed neatly in a grey suit, white stiff collar and dark tie, a smart grey hat upon his head and a great Edwardian moustache on his upper lip—at first black but greying with the years. He walks with an equally elegant Aunt Nell and his large shaggy dog, down neatly trimmed garden paths, through borders of flowers, past rustic trellises lush with climbing roses or, older now, he stands at a doorway, tall and straight, the patriarch of the family, between his white-haired sisters, Chattie and Elizabeth.

He is seen also in another photograph sitting on an iron bench beneath a tree with two impressive-looking gentlemen and another two behind him. The farmhouse is in the background. My father inscribed the names of these gentlemen in an album of old photographs which he assembled in his retirement. They were his uncles, two of them visiting from afar.

It would be interesting today to discover the communications that must have occurred in 1908 between Pasadena, California, Elphinstone, Manitoba, and Perth, Scotland. The Morton brothers in each place must have corresponded. All we know is that Andrew Morton sailed home across the Atlantic with his brother Robert, and we know the month was May and the year 1908. While they were in mid-Atlantic, their brother John died at the age of sixty-three. Perhaps John's illness was the reason for the trip. His death is the origin of a family story related in different places at different dates by my father, by the Elphinstone Mortons and by my Uncle John. Robert had left Scotland thirty-one years earlier, yet when he walked down the streets of Perth, he had the dubious distinction of finding strangers tipping their hats to him and muttering, "Good morning, Mr. Morton." They would then invariably stop short in alarm, realizing that Mr. Morton had just died. Like his brother John, Robert was a large stout, bearded man, hardly distinguishable from his deceased brother.

In the photograph, Robert's massive body sits there at one end of the bench, his fierce eyes piercing the camera. David, his moustache still black, sits more calmly at the other end, wearing a black bowler. And between them is the mighty Andrew, the then patriarch of the family, his legs crossed comfortably, both hands in his pockets, a cap on his head, his beard white and a great golden chain looping over his waistcoat. Look on my works, ye mighty, and despair. Andrew was sixty-five years of age, he had left the Muirton some forty-seven years earlier and if he had ever seen David before, it would have been only as an infant. My grandfather, James, had died seventeen years before. George was presumably in Dundee, but Thomas, over from Glasgow, stands serenely, slenderly aloof, behind the moguls on the bench, his hands in his pockets. Beside him stands a younger man, clean-shaven, wearing a clerical collar: the Reverend James Padkin. He had married Christian Morton, the fourteenth and last child of John and Helen, born in 1866 when her father was fifty-eight and her mother forty-nine years of age. These were the parents of Maymie Padkin Lindsay.

And who took the photograph? Perhaps it was Christian

Padkin, who must have been present with her eight-year-old daughter. Could it have been my father, at the age of twenty, perhaps even now delving into the mysteries of photography, as he most certainly did later?

But the guests departed for the New World, to resume their status as legends. Andrew had three children, all of whom visited their homeland at various times, though there is now no trace of them. The descendants of the two Elphinstone families, however, still visit the ancient land of their origins.

Little is known of James, the sixth son. Perhaps he was named after the Bowes side of the family since there is no record of a James on the Morton side. He was born in 1850 and is stated on my father's birth certificate to be a law cashier in Perth. On 29 December 1881 he married Margaret Taylor of Redgorton at the age of thirty-one years—a popular age for marriage in my ancestors—while his wife was a tender nineteen. They moved to Edinburgh where my Uncle John was born in 1882. A photograph taken of my grandfather in Edinburgh about this time shows him standing with the fingers of his left hand slid easily inside the pocket of his five-button jacket, a handsome top hat on his head. He wears muttonchops and a moustache. His face is round, his nose fine. His eyes are calm—as my father's could be—yet I expect them momentarily to flash fire and enthusiasm. Did he have the relaxed personality of my Uncle John or the vigorous, aggressive personality of my father? It is pleasing to look upon my grandfather.

At some time between 1882 and 1888 the family returned to Perth, for in that year a second son, Kenneth William, was born in Gannochyfold, Gannochy Road, a semidetached villa next to my grandmother's parents. James died in 1891, at forty-one, leaving two sons, aged nine and three years and a wife of twenty-nine years.

The boys attended school in Perth, performed their household tasks, carried their flagon of milk and a dozen eggs from the Muirton on a Saturday, and some summers were allowed a holiday on the Esperson Farm with Tom and Jim Lawrie. My father played rugby on the North Inch, walked upon Kinnoull Hill, rowed his boat up the Tay and into the Sawmill Stream with his friend Bob Clark—and attended classes in Dundee, while his brother became an estate agent.

From this point there is a gap in my knowledge of my father's life—until I looked up and saw his strong, hard hands grasping the wooden steering wheel of the McLaughlin Buick as it bounced over the potholes on Fourteenth Avenue.

My father always managed to keep himself occupied during his retirement. He kept contact with his profession by being on the North Fraser Harbour Commission, but he spent most of his time in his garden or in his basement where he now had power saws and planers to build furniture for his three married children. He also built a greenhouse, for, as he said, he could do a better job than anyone he could hire. In actuality, perhaps the challenge meant more to him, as well as the feeling of accomplishment when he stood back and saw the work completed.

He acted as a chauffeur on the frequent shopping expeditions organized by Flo Doran and my mother, neither of whom over the years had expressed the slightest interest in solving the intricacies of the modern motor car. It was in this period that Flo made an eventful, and what must have been to her a terrifying, decision. Em had died suddenly in 1953. She lived alone in that great house of a hundred gables, but in 1955 she sold it. No one dared asked her why she did so, though it must have been out of absolute and complete necessity. In her stolid manner, she showed no emotion. She purchased a small cottage on the Grandview-Douglas Highway (now Canada Way) hardly a hundred yards from my parents' house. It was on the land once occupied by Eulice Dowd's vast chicken runs.

I do not know how Flo disposed of the massive accumulation of bric-a-brac that the family had gathered over fifty years. I do know, however, that it caused deep pain in her lonely soul and I do know that the house was virtually empty when I drove over to help her on her last evening there. I parked my car in the vacant lot where my father used to park the McLaughlin Buick, and walked under the cherry tree, past the mossy letters that read Lorne Villa and up the three steps to the long, wide, cool verandah. The mechanical bell tinkled very faintly now, but Flo appeared and I entered her home for the last time. She was just a little flustered that evening, though it seemed to be more from concern for my time than for her last moments in her home. Everything movable in the rambling old mansion had disappeared. It was as if Flo wished to erase the last vestige of her existence in that ancient home. I filled the car with the remaining articles and when I returned, Flo was frantically tearing the carpet from the staircase that led down to the hall. It was madness—the carpet was useless—but it was something that could be moved. I pulled it away from the stairs, rolled it and placed it in the car. There was just one more thing, Flo said. Would I mind chopping up her kitchen table? The act of destroying is never pleasant, but Flo asked me and I did it. I took Em's great double-bladed axe and I desperately split and slashed and chopped that heavy, solid fir table into little bits, and I felt like weeping as I piled the remains at the bottom of the back steps.

I walked into the hall and up the steps to look again at the balcony, but the door was locked and I did not ask Flo for the key. The halls on the second floor echoed to my tread and the back stairs to the kitchen creaked. Downstairs Flo had on her tweed coat and she was tucking her hair beneath her broad-brimmed felt hat, stuck squarely on her head. She handed me the gong and leather-headed mallet I had enjoyed so much as a child. "I thought you might like this," she said quickly and turned away. "That's all now." She closed the front door behind her, locked it and walked away without the slightest sign of emotion, as if we were setting off on her regular Friday trip to the market.

I drove her to her new home, carried everything into her

house—already crammed solidly with memorabilia—and left her alone. What else could one do? She must have been shocked and hurt and dismayed—but it was just as if she had returned from the market.

She never saw her old home again. On one of their shopping expeditions, my father drove down Fourteenth Avenue and turned up Kingsway. Flo bowed her head and closed her eyes tightly. She would not look at her home. Not a word was spoken, but my father never again took that route when Flo was with him.

Flora McCulloch Doran continued her regular way of life, though many adaptations had to be made after the deaths of my mother and father. She showed no external emotion to these events, and no one ever knew the secret feelings in her proud Scottish heart. She died alone in her crowded little cottage on Douglas Road. If she had had her choice, I am sure that she would have preferred to have been cremated with her possessions and her cottage on the very spot where she died. There was no one left. By then the house of a hundred gables had been torn to shreds by a hard-hatted man on a monster machine.

There is a drive-in restaurant on part of the property now, but the greater portion is wasteland. Yet I can still see the storm-tossed roof—I can still see "Lorne Villa" pressed into the weathered concrete walk, the great broad verandah, the floating balcony and the beautiful garden of that magnificent home on Kingsway. I can still see Mi-cah's sweet face on the balcony with Flo and Isabel and Em and my father and mother sitting peacefully there on a warm Sunday afternoon in summer.

My father saw four grandsons and a granddaughter before he died suddenly and alone in his home on 31 March 1959, in his seventieth year. On the day of his funeral I went to his old desk, removed the two diaries I knew were there and did not tell my mother until they were safely in my own home. She was aghast, but submitted when I promised I would not read them while she still lived.

My mother remained alone in that large house on Fourteenth Avenue, though she did not survive for long. Like my father, she died suddenly in her home on 24 November 1960. The next day my daughter was born, and I opened the first volume of my father's diary.

I have a strange sensation that my life has been little more than a series of flashbacks. It began unobtrusively in 1922 and progressed in a somewhat orderly fashion until 1951 when I began to look over my shoulder—and in 1953 it suddenly reverted to 1755 when my great-great-great-grandfather John married Christian Miller. I lived through those years of the Gallowmuir, the Muirton and the fourteen children—the years of Boswell, Johnson, Garrick, Burns and Scott—and my curiosity was satisfied, but only temporarily. I could not shake the past. My father filled a few of the many gaps in the family history that I wrote before his death, pressing his remarks deeply into his pad of pink paper. I was unable to get any more information until my mother died and I could read my father's diary. Suddenly I was back again in the first decade of the century.

My father is two months past his twentieth birthday when Jimmy and Tommy Lawrie visit him for the New Year holiday in 1909. With John, my uncle, they walk, talk, fire their rifles in the woods and are entranced by *The Merry Widow* in the local theatre. But the Lawrie boys depart on the fourth day of January and my father is "dashed sorry." I have never heard him use this expression.

The holidays are over now and he must return to his regular life, which is not at all a drudgery to him. He seems to enjoy every moment of it. He has finished his formal schooling at University College, where he gained four first- and four second-class honours, and has been an apprentice in the office of Blackadder and Allan, civil engineers, in Dundee, for almost two years. Each morning my father rises at six o'clock, lights the fire in the kitchen grate, takes his mother her cup of tea in bed, makes his own breakfast, slaps his cap on his head and sets off for the Dundee train, a little over a mile away. He steps aboard the eight o'clock train and settles back to watch the young ladies on the platform or, preferably, in his carriage. He is, it seems, an inveterate ogler. He doffs his cap to them, smiles and may even mutter, "Good morning," but that is all, for he has not been formally introduced to them. He does not know their names, though he has labelled all the regulars. There is, for instance, the Glencarse girl and the Errol girl, since they board the train in these towns in the morning, and there is the Keillor girl, since she works at the large jam factory in Dundee. There is also a very proper young lady whom my father has delightfully named Miss Prim, since when he gazes at her, she will not return his glance but stares straight ahead in her pristine purity. But even when he is formally introduced to a young lady, he still refers to her as Miss Young or Miss Stewart.

As the train winds down beside the Tay, he might read a text on mechanics or copy some notes, but he is much more engrossed in the sock he is knitting. On the train? In front of the Glencarse girl and the Errol girl? I knew, of course, that he could knit, for once, long ago, each member of our family knitted at least one square of an Afghan rug made of spare pieces of wool, and I once knitted a sweater—but in the privacy of our home, not in front of Miss Prim. He even knits in the draughting room when he has some spare time, and here Miss Stewart, a lusty jade, it seems, teaches him how to turn the heel. He quickly progresses down the foot, takes in at the toes, casts off, tries it on and is shattered to find the foot is too short. He had started it on December 24, finished it on February 22— and now he unravels the toe, adds a few inches, takes it in, casts off and it fits nicely this time. The second sock progresses more quickly and my father is extemely pleased when he turns the heel without the aid of Miss Stewart.

Through the day he works on his perspective, plans a sewage system or perhaps travels with his boss, Blackadder, to Glamis or Kerrie to assist in a survey. He catches the five o'clock train back to Perth, studies the theory of mechanics or Fidler's *Deflection of Beams,* has supper between eight and nine and goes to bed.

Saturdays begin the same as any other day of the week, but he escapes from the Dundee office on the run at 1:00 P.M. and the rest of the day seems always to be a mad rush, for my father is a rugby enthusiast. I knew that, of course. He used to stand at one end of our tennis lawn and drop-kick the ball to the neighbourhood children waiting at the other end and often it would sail high over the fence and out to Fourteenth Avenue. But in 1909 he races for a train to Kirkcaldy or Glen Almond or St. Andrews—or even home to the North Inch— where he glories in his triumphs and agonizes in his defeats. In St. Andrews, "I had a beautiful drop goal," he boasts. "My face was to my own goal and I put a big screw on it and it touched the near post and went inside." But he blames himself for two tries the opposing side makes, and the moment the match is over, he rushes with his friend, Jimmy Christie, to the train— only to find it pulling out of the station. The two young men collapse with exhaustion and disappointment, but the train stops again for another passenger and they manage to revive themselves, rush on and climb into the carriage as the train moves away. My father is, he says, "fair out of wind." And he adds a few words of penance. "I never swore so much as when I saw that train move out and I thank God for forgiving me and letting me get it after shaming his name."

He walks the mile home from the station, washes himself and walks a further three miles back across the river and out the Dunkeld Road to the North Muirton. He has supper there at eight—the first food he has had since breakfast; he kills two cocks and carries them home, where he tumbles into bed "feeling dashed tired." This is my father who for so much of his life used to slip a tablet of nitroglycerin beneath his tongue.

Tea and supper at the Muirton, North or South and sometimes both, are invariable features of every Saturday. Here we meet Uncle David and Aunt Nell on the North, as well as various servants and ploughmen. Aunts Chattie and Lizzie we see on the South. But wait, there is also an "Uncle A." living at the South. Could it be Andrew? He had arrived in May of the year before. Has he overstayed his welcome? It is indeed Andrew, for my father ultimately mentions him by name. Andrew Morton of Pasadena, California. Here he sits before us in the pages of my father's diary: the family enigma, the alleged skeleton in the family closet. Andrew, the eldest child, who left home in his teens, surely under unpleasant circumstances, almost fifty years earlier, to wander the world and become a wealthy man. Has he seen the will in which his father, John, decreed that, should Andrew object, he would forfeit his share of the estate? If he has, perhaps he chuckled to himself. He has no need of old John's money nor his farm. Yet he is still here, dallying after eight months. He must be enjoying himself. Or perhaps he is lonesome in California. There is a family rumour that his wife, Julia, committed suicide after the birth of their last child, and perhaps his children have grown up and have left home. It is difficult to decide whether my father takes him seriously or not. One evening after supper at the North Muirton, my father walks to the South with his American uncle and on the way "gets a lecture on the stars." And when "the South people" visit Gannochyfold for tea, "Uncle Andrew says sermons should be lectures on popular subjects such as farming." My father answers, "I say we should learn this through the week," and a long discussion ensues. Andrew remains an enigma. Does he pay rent on the South? Do his sisters, Chattie and Lizzie, cook his meals and wash his clothes?

Perhaps this is too much to expect my father to record. He sits in the North Muirton farmhouse on a Saturday evening playing Pop-in-Law, dominoes or nap with his Uncle Andrew. But on the evening of March 16 he says good-bye to him, not expecting to see him again, yet early on the eighteenth, he cuts the ivy around his mother's home and then: "To the station and saw Uncles David and Andrew and talked till train time then said good-bye and Uncle Andrew threw kisses in passing and seemed sorry to leave. Uncle David said he may be coming to live in Scotland." Andrew passes from the scene, to be heard from later only by postcard.

Uncle David is perhaps less affable, judging from such remarks referring to his being talkative one evening or in a good mood another. My father, the opportunist, takes advantage of the latter to remind his uncle that Gannochyfold must have a load of dung this month (March). Two weeks later Uncle David admits voluntarily that he has not yet sent the dung and my father, in the somewhat pointed manner I know so well, answers, "No you haven't." The delivery of two loads of dung—one horse, the other cow—is a constantly recurring subject that spring.

Then there is Aunt Nell, David's wife. She is a kind soul. She slips a sixpence into Kenneth's or John's hand whenever possible, or perhaps a dozen eggs—indeed, one evening my father carries home six eggs, a bag of tatties and a flagon of milk and arrives completely fatigued, more from the fear of breaking the eggs than from the weight of his burden. Often Aunt Nell is in bed when he visits the Muirton and on some occasions my father remarks that she is "foo'." It is not until the end of May that the terrible truth is recorded openly in his diary. His mother, Uncle David and Aunt Nell go to Edinburgh in search of another servant. My father meets them on their return in the evening ". . . and Aunt Nell had evidently been mortal drunk in Edinburgh and they had an awful time." My mother and father have told me many wonderful tales of their youth, but this one they must have conveniently forgotten—and I feel deeply for my strait-laced grandmother and more deeply for Uncle David, who surely can be excused for his swings of mood. It is a family disaster, yet everyone seems to live graciously with it. And her illness does not detract from Aunt

Nell. She has a big heart. She gives my father a pound note so he can go to a students' dinner in Glasgow, but his mother will not give her assent, though she later relents.

And on Sunday there is church in the morning and church in the evening, followed by bible class where one might see projected views of Jerusalem or the plan of a synagogue. My father sits in the pew of the North Church—where I sat in 1951—and he seems to pay more attention to the young ladies of the congregation than to the Reverend Millar Patrick, particularly to two young ladies. Since he does not know their first names, he refers to them as Murdoch 2 and Murdoch 3—my mother and my aunt, aged eighteen and seventeen. He tries to catch their eye and sometimes succeeds, but all too often "mamma" or "papa" are watching too closely. My father, however, surely also listens, since he records the subject of each sermon and a brief summary, occasionally adding his own remarks. And in between services he walks with his friends Bob Clark or Jimmy Christie on Kinnoull or Corsie Hill or on the North Inch.

Of his mother and brother there are few revealing remarks. There is sometimes a family spat, though it seems to be a reasonably pleasant household. John, twenty-seven years of age, belongs to the militia, an interest he retained till the end of his days. He and my father talk for an hour one evening on the subject of life in the army; once John attends a military dance, and in the summer he goes off to army camp. It is strange to think of my Uncle John at a dance; he once told me he had danced but a few times in his life. One evening my father is digging diligently in the family garden and notes that John stands by, talking; and on another, "John took huff because he couldn't get the dung up the garden. I told him to leave me and I took it up myself. John ploutered about and mother in a terrible rage when he went to brigade and told him he needn't come back." The incident, like most family quarrels, was soon forgotten, though my father adds, "John did come back."

Sometimes his mother is in a bad temper, but her younger son still serves her tea in bed before he leaves for Dundee in the morning, and in the evening he often reads to her, on one occasion, three full chapters of *Clementina*.

In the spring, however, his mind is constantly on his garden, though this never replaces his interest in the young ladies of the town. As early as January he purchases the monthly magazine *Gardening* and in February he is preparing a bed for a boxwood hedge which he plans to buy. He haggles with a Dundee nurseryman but cannot come to a fair price, and at the same time he is after his Uncle David again to send the dung. My father was certainly a persistent young man. Surely his Uncle David must have had to restrain himself from chastising his aggressive nephew who seems constantly to be nagging at him. The dung finally arrives at Gannochyfold, but, alas, it is cow dung and my father insists on horse. The second load, this time horse dung, finally arrives and the great dung controversy is thankfully over. Perhaps he insists on this brand since he is preparing a mushroom bed.

In the meantime, the haggling over the price of a boxwood hedge continues. It is finally settled, and early in April a great box of bushes is loaded onto the train in Glencarse. When he sees it sitting on the platform in Perth station, he is surprised at its size and weight. "But no way for it," he says, "but to carry it, so I swing it on my shoulder and down Marshall Place to the bridge, then rested, then to Cameron's and got a barrow and burled it up the rest, fair pouring of sweat." Over the next few days, he and John plant it along the garden walk. He gets his tatties planted early in April and begins his next project, the construction of a cold frame. Frequently he arises very early, works on the frame, has breakfast, travels to Dundee and returns in the evening to plane the wood he carried from the Muirton. He then starts the corner dovetails. Dovetails? To me, this sounds quite unnecessary—a few nails here and there would be quite sufficient—but not for my father. (In the 1950s, he built me a cold frame of thick tongue-and-groove cedar, and he dovetailed the four corners. It is still in my garden more than twenty years later.) And then he goes on a buying spree for seeds—cress mustard, lettuce, tomatoes, wallflower, pansies, carnations, stocks, asters, lobelia, calceolaria. His sweet peas are up by then and he hikes off to Corsie Hill to find stakes—and he fears that he will never get down to studying for his exams until the garden is in.

Why does my father work so hard? My mother used to tell him he had done enough for today. "Leave some for tomorrow," she would say; but he never could, it seems. One Sunday evening he comes home from church, cleans out the dining room, lifts the carpet—and confides in his diary, with just a trace of guilt, that this is "fine work for Sunday." The next morning he is up especially early to beat the carpet, clean the chairs and polish the piano, and the reason for this great burst of housework, as it later develops, is that Mrs. Lawrie and her daughter, Jean, are about to arrive from Esperson for a visit. But my father is also deeply involved in developing his own photographs now, and after he prints them, he places them on a mirror to obtain a glossy finish. I had forgotten that. When I was young he used to cover my mother's full-length mirror with photographs in their wet stage—and my mother would feign annoyance.

Now what is this? Another controversy? He is haggling with a man in Dundee over the price of a rowboat—an argument as endless as the great dung debate and the battle of the boxwood hedge. The price is three pounds, ten shillings without oars and he notes there is a good two pounds of repairs to be done, with an additional pound for oars. He offers thirty shillings and departs when it is refused, but he is back a few days later, still haggling and still departing stubbornly, until finally the deal is made—three pounds, five shillings and four pence, with a pair of second-hand oars thrown in.

The boat is towed the twenty miles up the Tay to Perth on

the high tide and there my father takes it on her maiden voyage, only to find that it leaks and that the oars are too long. He sinks it, in the hope of tightening the planks, but this ploy fails so he obtains some white lead and hemp to repair the seams. This job, he finds, is impossible to do on the banks of the river, and as he cannot afford three shillings to rent a lorry, he borrows a horse and cart at 5:00 A.M., when it can be had more cheaply, and trundles the boat home with Jimmy Christie who, along with Bob Clark, is part-owner. But it is my father who does all the work. He fills the seams, constructs backs for the stern and bow seats and repairs the rudder, most of this early in the morning before breakfast. And finally in July he has the pleasure of taking his mother for a row up the Tay. The tide is so high that they reach Woody Island, the eastern border of the Muirton.

All this time he is also working in the garden. He must have bought too many wallflower seeds—or perhaps every single one germinated—for he transplants fifteen dozen into the area where the first tattie crop has been harvested. He surely told me this, for I remember telling Uncle John, that evening when he had me slave in his Comiston Road garden, that my father used to grow wallflowers at Gannochyfold. And he trims the hedges, cuts the green at Gannochyfold and occasionally at the Muirton, repairs his fishing rod, soles his boots and tries valiantly to study. And even now he is looking for a job. In March he travels to Glasgow where several firms tell him there is nothing available, and in July he visits Edinburgh and is told that all the jobs are in Glasgow. He is "awfully wearied," but he returns home to find his garden flourishing, and he delights in his first three mushrooms.

For the first two weeks of August my father visits the Lawries at the Esperson Farm and there are no diary entries. He begins again on the day he leaves, a Saturday, and on the Monday he is back at work in Dundee. In the mornings and evenings he paints the inside and outside of his boat and adds

several coats of varnish. He cuts and crushes rhubarb in preparation for wine, covers forty-three pots of jam with paraffin
wax, prunes trees and works in the garden. In September he
travels to St. Andrews armed with a testimonial from Professor
Claxton Fidler, his old teacher and author of several engineering texts, but even this approach fails and he becomes more and
more discouraged. There are only two bright spots in his existence at this time—the resumption of the rugby season and the
information, supplied by a friend, that Murdochs 1, 2 and 3 are
named Isa, Nellie and Elsie, and he wishes he knew Nellie. A
roller-skating rink opens in Perth, and in early October he slips
out of the house while his mother is away, expecting to be back
by 9:30; but he escorts a young lady home and when he reaches
Gannochyfold at 10:30, his mother is waiting for him, terribly
angry—and he says that he knows he deserves her anger. He is
more discouraged than ever and he prays that God will help
him. The next morning he serves his mother tea in bed, prepares breakfast of hard, thick porridge and is angry at John for
being so lazy. Suddenly everything has deteriorated. I have
never known my father so depressed.

There are also family problems at this time. My father sees
his cousin Jean and Aunt Nell at Perth station, and his aunt is
"spiffed." On his Saturday evening visits to the Muirton she is
frequently "ill" or "in bed," and when his mother and Aunt
Nell attend Aunt Bell's funeral on the outskirts of Dundee, he
underlines his remark that Aunt Nell was ill—and I wonder if
this is the reason for my father's great antipathy for the demon
alcohol.

Early in October, however, he is obsessed with thoughts of a
coming party. He talks to his friends about it, speculates on
who is going, where they will meet and when they will appear.
There is a strange and unnatural concern about the event. It is
not until the thirteenth, the day of the party, that he reveals
the site. It is the church hall—and suddenly the reason for his
concern is evident. He arrives sufficiently early to observe who
is there and where they are sitting, he hangs his coat in the

vestry and proceeds out into the hall feeling "unhandy." He works his way over to where Nellie and Elsie Murdoch are sitting and, without being too obvious, sits as close to them as possible. The 100th Psalm is read followed by a prayer—and then the minister announces that mere attendance at this gathering can be considered an introduction to anyone in the hall. Is my very existence dependent upon this trivial announcement made by the Reverend Millar Patrick in 1909? I am very nearly a victim of Victorian formality.

Following tea there is a little concert. Elsie Murdoch steps up to the stage and recites "The Aspinall's at Home," and is followed by an ugly soprano, as judged by my father. There are then a series of games such as Armless Chairs and Pass the Penny, and somehow my father contrives always to have as his partner one of the Murdoch girls. He has a magnificent time, and after the doxology he asks Elsie if she is going home with anyone. She answers yes, with her sister—which is precisely what my father knew she would say. He walks up Balhousie Street with them, "Nellie looking rare in a rough cloth coat, Elsie in red." They chatter away happily and Elsie says she never knew my father's name until this very evening. Now this I do not believe. I knew my Auntie Elsie and my Uncle Andy very well, and he was at that very party; and forty years later, after my aunt had related a long and involved though exciting tale—she had a gift for fashioning a good story—Uncle Andy sat back in his chair in Battersea and growled through his pipe that the Murdochs were all great embellishers. I am certain that both girls knew my father's name.

It does not matter. It is merely a vignette of three—four—people I knew so well and loved. And there are few who can say they saw their mother and father meet for the first time. He sees the girls to the very gate of Dunearn and walks home in ecstasy. He lies in bed, sleepless, hearing the downstairs clock ring one, then two, then three o'clock before he finally falls asleep—only to dream of Murdochs.

Now this tale was not meant to deteriorate into a romance.

I merely read my father's diary because I wanted to know more about him. How was I to know that in it he met my mother on 13 October 1909 and could talk of little else until the second volume stutters through partial entries and finally succumbs on a blank page? And it is now more difficult for me to read the diary since my father's life is so full that he must write in a microscopic hand and my aging eyes require a magnifying glass.

Every morning he plans his route and his hour of travel to coincide with the habit of Nellie Murdoch. Every evening he times his return from Dundee so he can meet Nellie as she walks home from the General Accident Insurance office on Tay Street "the G.A." of which my mother often spoke where she was a stenographer. Often he is foiled, since she is walking with a companion, though always he receives a smile; but equally often he stops and talks. He can do so now. He has been introduced by the magnanimous, though fortuitous, gesture of the Reverend Millar Patrick to whom I owe my existence on the glorious thirteenth. There of course can be no suggestion of a "date" in the modern sense. He must meet her only accidentally on the street, or on the North Inch, perhaps up Kinnoull Hill, and certainly at any church function. They do, however, cheat a little on their parents by her allowing it to be known where she will be at a certain hour or a certain day: shopping on the High Street, a music lesson at Mr. Graves's and "Quoir" practice. Though they dare not consider their meetings as such, they are clandestine trysts. He skates with her at the roller rink; she apologizes profusely for giving him so much trouble when her skate comes off three times, but he is delighted. She feigns embarrassment—my mother was a great feigner—when he tells her he will be in the theatre to hear her sing in an operetta since, she says, she will be "painted." And indeed she is, but he cannot take his eyes from her. The next night he meets her at the stage door, hands her a bunch of violets and walks home with her and Elsie, who is also in the operetta. He wheedles a photograph from each of them, dressed in their costumes, photographs that I have stored away in my home. And the next evening he sends Nellie an anonymous gift of a box of chocolates by way of Mr. Graves, her voice teacher, delivered to his house by a child who receives from my father the sum of one penny for his efforts. There is a great deal of intrigue over who this anonymous admirer is and finally all is revealed. And so the romance continues—at least in my father's eyes—though he is aware that there is at least one other suitor for her hand.

On 12 November 1909 my father prints neatly below the date in his diary, "Birthday 21." It is the same as any other day. He serves his mother tea in bed, prepares breakfast and works in the Dundee office, but he returns in time for tea at Bob Clark's. They play bagatelle, sing a few songs, and Bob leaves him for a moment to return with a book and a knife. His brother, Gordie, appears with a book, and Mrs. Clark presents him with a silver-mounted cherrywood walking stick. A silver-mounted cherrywood walking stick? There is something familiar about this description. Surely it could not be the one my son played with when he was very young and later used in a school play? I find it at the back of a closet in our home and indeed it is a silver-mounted cherrywood walking stick. I cannot believe it. I can remember once my father using it on a Sunday walk when I was small and thinking how ridiculous it was for a perfectly healthy man to use a cane. I can see my son strutting about the house with it, though I do not know how it got here. It is one of three presents my father received on his twenty-first birthday. There were no others.

My father's life revolves around his clandestine romance. He does his garden and household chores, repairs the handle of a spade, prepares the vegetables for dinner, makes a pudding, cleans the grate, puts a door handle, a lock and an incandescent lamp "in order" and helps at the Muirton on Saturdays, but his life is full of romantic intrigues, many of them arranged by my beloved Auntie Elsie—"a ripping girl," my father says—though these young people are somewhat tiring with their constant polite conversations, imagined slights, apologies and accidental trysts.

There is only one other event worthy of my father's attention. He is awarded his cap for rugby for Perth; it is retroactive to 1907 and runs through 1908 and 1909. He orders it from the firm of Gow and Murdoch on John Street and when it arrives in December, he wears it proudly around the North Inch. My grandfather's firm made a very good job of it. Though today the silver embossing is tarnished, the velvet shows no signs of its seventy years. My grandfather, whom I never met, held it in his hands; my father wore it as a raw youth, and my mother, hardly a sports enthusiast, expressed her admiration of it as it sat upon the bold young head of Kenneth Morton.

December 24 is an ordinary day except that John goes to a sergeant's dance in the evening, and December 25 is little different. My father has sent a few Christmas cards, but he rises at 8:30, has nothing to do so cuts "sticks" for the stove, then watches a curling match in town. In the afternoon he goes to the roller-skating rink and skates with Isa, Elsie and Nellie Murdoch, proceeds to the North Muirton where Aunt Nell is "half-spiffed" and is in bed by 10:00. How different his Christmases would be in Canada—surely this was one of his easiest adaptations. And it is at this time, on 31 December 1909, that he first mentions emigration. He tells his ladylove that if he passes his exams, he will go abroad next summer, and to his great delight she gasps, "Oh!"

The four-day New Year holiday is no more exciting than Christmas. My father plays rugby on the North Inch on Saturday, the first day of 1910, attends church and visits the Muirton. A few days later he is off to Corsie Hill to find pine trees for a bower which he plans to build in the garden. At dawn he stands upon the peak and gazes with pleasure on the soft glow of the morning sky and the sun, just beginning to appear above the hills to the east. It is so silent that he fears snapping a branch lest it wake up the whole world. My father hears the sounds of silence, just as I did at Mount Gardner, though I did not give him credit for such sensitivity. But he rouses himself, selects three large pines and drags them behind him all the way home, wondering why the ploughmen in Ballingall's fields stare at him so strangely. Twenty years later he would pull a great raft of cedars from Cariboo Road behind the McLaughlin Buick to build the rustic fence along Fourteenth Avenue— and no doubt the residents of East Burnaby stared at him in a similar manner. Every morning before work, if the weather is reasonable, he saws and chips and fits the half-lap joints together and makes further trips to Corsie until the bower is complete and looks "just fine."

Mid-January, however, is a troubled period. He is bored with the office. His mother catches John smoking in the back garden—he is now twenty-eight—and there is a terrible row. At the door of the church my father raises his cap to Nellie Murdoch; his mother later asks who she is and when told, criticizes her at great length, much to my father's annoyance. He does not record the criticism, yet it is a well-known fact in our family that our grandmother had no use for our mother. Perhaps it was because she sang on the stage. I will never know. I do not believe the two ever met.

And even the weather becomes terribly cold. The Tay freezes and on January 22 my father goes ice skating on the quarry pond. On the last round of the day, his skates get tangled with a friend's, they fall and the point of a skate pierces my father's left calf. Blood flows freely, a tourniquet is applied, and he is taken to his home in a cab where a doctor dresses and bandages it. But the leg injury is only part of his anguish. For weeks he has been looking forward to a concert at which Nellie Murdoch will sing—and early in February he must travel to London to write his Institute of Civil Engineering examinations.

It is strange to read of this accident. I can remember the tale from the mists of my childhood. My father told it with his usual enthusiasm, smiling and laughing and pointing to the very spot where the skate pierced his calf. He did not mention his anguish, the heartache and frustration of sitting alone all day in the house studying, or "sorting" the parlour clock, frantic at the thought of missing the concert. In desperation he writes a note to Nellie, asks John to slip it into her hand at church and feels better, in spite of taking the terrible chance that John might be caught in the act, in which case his reputation would be in ruins. To his great delight, John returns to tell a harrowing tale of the difficulties he experienced, but with his mission completed. "Hurrah for John!" my father writes. "He's a dinger!" He is confined to the house for ten days, then limps into town and meets his lady who shows great concern over his injury; and he is extremely happy again. The turbulent world of youth.

Sunday, 6 February 1910 is a rather emotional day for my father. He attends morning and evening services as well as bible class, walks home with the Murdoch girls to the very gate of Dunearn, experiences uneasiness at the thought of leaving home, and wonders how he will feel if he goes abroad. It is a strange response. He is, after all, going to be away for only a week, and he has been away previously for as long as two weeks—to Esperson, just a few miles to the south of Edinburgh. But on this occasion he is crossing the border to a foreign country—to England, to London. His only solace is that he will be back in a week, in time for the bible class social.

He takes a cab to Perth station in the morning, carrying Aunt Nell's travelling bag as well as ten shillings from both Aunt Chattie and Aunt Liz, seven and six from Aunt Nell and two pounds from Uncle David. His heartstrings pull as the train puffs out of the station at 8:30, but he soon recovers enough to enjoy a fleeting glimpse of the great cities of Newcastle, York, Durham and Doncaster. He is in London by 6:30 that evening and is met by his cousin Jock Young. They go on to Teddington where my father is to stay with Jock and a group of young men while he writes his engineering exams. They sing and talk, and when he goes to bed he feels strange with so many people about—and a trifle guilty at not having the nerve to recite his prayers publicly.

He has a free day on the eighth but on the ninth he finds his way to South Kensington and writes Mechanics, then Strength of Materials, and "got on rare," though the two papers the following day are "stiff." That evening he meets Georgie, to whom he has previously written. She is presumably a Perth girl since she knows his mother. They walk past the Albert Memorial, have tea in Lyons' and attend the Empire Theatre. Unfortunately, however, "she talks quite English," as my father says (and if there was anything worse than a Scot acquiring an English accent, it was a Canadian doing the same). Georgie excuses herself by pointing out that the children she teaches could not understand her if she spoke otherwise.

His last exam is the following morning, after which he glances briefly at Piccadilly Circus and sees *Carmen* in the Kingston Theatre. He meets Georgie briefly the next day, and Jock shows him St. Paul's, the Embankment, Westminster and Buckingham Palace.

He spends the last day in London with the fair Georgie. My father was a rogue. Has he forgotten my mother? They walk to Kew Gardens where he takes a number of photographs. I open the old album that my father assembled in his retirement and there they are, though Georgie has been diplomatically expunged. Previously they had meant nothing to me, yet here is my father describing them a decade before I was born. Here also are the five young men with whom he stayed, three of them with pipes jutting from the sides of their mouths, dressed in suits and waistcoats, a group of dandies.

But Georgie? Why, my father holds her hand, puts his arm over her shoulder as they sit on a bench beside the river and finally he kisses her—and thinks of Nellie. Have you ever kissed

a girl and thought of someone else? He shakes hands with her—
have you ever shaken hands with a girl you have just kissed?—
says he might be going to Canada in the spring, and leaves poor
Georgie "perhaps for the last time in this world."

The train speeds north from King's Cross, arrives in Perth
three minutes early, and he goes immediately to the bible class
social where he plays Advertisements and Pass the Orange and
takes part in *The Merry Miller* with the Murdoch girls. Nellie
sings "Bridge of Allan Water," but, alas, someone else sees her
home. Perhaps my father deserves it.

Before you know it, we are into the dung season again,
though it is not as prolonged an episode as in the previous year.
A load of cow and a load of horse dung arrive in the first week
of February. There is also the usual spring activity in the
garden. My father buys a Dorothy Perkins rose for the bower,
reads *Gardening* magazine and begins to cultivate his
wallflowers again. He is most pleased with himself when he
receives postcards from both Elsie and Nellie from Glasgow,
where they are visiting, though his mother sees them and is
obviously not pleased. "There seems to be a run on the Murdochs now," she remarks and my father is "roused." On two
occasions his mother refers to Nellie as "tubular looking," and
my father wonders if she suspects he is quite keen on Murdoch
2. On another occasion his mother angrily says, when he is a
little late getting home, that he prefers the Murdochs to her.
He makes no comment. Was my grandmother possessive of her
younger son? She is certainly strict, perhaps tyrannical, even
puritanical. There was, as we have seen, a terrible row when
she caught John smoking in the garden and my father is always
in fear that she will catch him, though he smokes little. He
records every cigarette, generally about four or five a week. But
even when he gets "roused" at his mother, he treats her
remarkably well. He still brings her tea in bed, often makes
dinner, bakes puddings or pancakes or omelettes, reads to her in
the evening, and prays nightly for a job so that he can help his

mother. When he meets his mother, Uncle David and Aunt Nell accidentally at Perth station, he writes, "It's as bad as I've ever seen Aunt Nell. She came down on Mother's and the servant's arms. It's a shame to make Mother do it and I felt dashed roused. Saw Mother after they'd got her into the train and Uncle David looked very worried."

Yet his mother appears to have quite a pleasant life. She is often away for one or two weeks at a time in Edinburgh, Glasgow, Esperson or Strathmiglo, and just prior to her return my father cleans the house from top to bottom, has a steam pudding ready and the tea set.

And spring brings renewed interest in the rowboat. He paints and varnishes it, fixes the floorboards and finally launches her. Elsie Murdoch is assigned the job of thinking of a name and for several weeks there is great intrigue over the one she has chosen. She tells my father it is a flower—which is ultimately revealed as a combination of the names of the three Murdoch lassies. It is *Nelsa*. In my childhood, my father was so pleased with this name that I always believed he had devised it.

There are glorious moments while he rows the Murdoch girls up the river, but then he is suddenly spurned by his ladylove, for no specific reason other than that it is a whim of the feminine gender. Elsie says her sister can never make up her mind and my father prays that she will cease her swithering and settle on him. He is terribly depressed. "God's will, not mine, be done," he writes, as he always does when he is worried; yet it is little comfort. I sympathize with him though I find it difficult to be too concerned. I know it will turn out well, whether by the grace of God, the luck of the swither or the ambitions of the Kaiser Wilhelm. To my father it is 1910, and he does not know what will happen tomorrow, far less nine or ten years from then. He is devastated, but the intrigues go on and on and on, as they do in every generation of youth. My father was no exception.

He works in the office, knits a tie, mends his boots, cultivates the garden and rows his boat—at least until his partner, Bob Clark, holes it badly on a rock in the river. They pull her up on the Cowslip Bank on the North Inch and my father cuts away the broken plank, finds a replacement, cuts it, fits it, presses it into place and achieves such a tight fit that the white lead squeezes out on all sides. He is annoyed at Bob either for not appearing to help or for not helping when he appears. But I sympathize with Bob, seventy years later; my father liked to do things himself and he liked perfection. But in spite of holed rowboats and broken romances, life goes on—indeed, Edward VII dies at this time and George V is proclaimed king. John finds a job in Doune, and though my father applies for several positions, nothing is available and he frequently contemplates Canada. Towards the end of June, however, the city of Cowdenbeath, a mining town in Fife and an hour's journey south of Perth, hires him for a three- or four-week period "at 30 shillings a week and digs and board of 15 shillings." It is not much but it is a start.

Did you know that p.p.c.s were extremely popular in my father's day? Whenever one left town for even a day, one would send a picture postcard to his dearest friends. My father kept the postie busy, particularly the fellow who carried the mail to the General Accident Insurance office where Nellie Murdoch worked. It was, after all, too dangerous to write directly to Duncarn on Balhousie Street. It is remarkable, too, to note that he could mail a p.p.c. in the evening and be assured that it would be delivered in Perth by 2:00 P.M. the next day.

My father's first day of work is July 4—a date that nine years later would be his wedding day—and the job lasts until September 4. He works from eight in the morning until nine or ten at night, and he is no more reticent about demanding extra pay for extra work from his boss than he is in demanding horse dung from his Uncle David. He succeeds in getting another five shillings. Some weekends he returns to Perth. He purchases cricket pads from Joe Anderson and plays on the North Inch. He works in the garden and relentlessly pursues his failing romance with limited success. He has at least gained the attention of Mr. Murdoch, the dapper tailor of John Street, who at first acknowledges him with a nod, progresses to a "How d'you do" and finally speaks to my father outside the North Church. It suddenly starts to rain and Mr. Murdoch remarks to my father that Nellie and Elsie are off somewhere with their brother, Will ". . . and the brats haven't taken umbrellas." My mother and beloved aunt referred to as brats? But it was gracious of my grandfather to speak to my father, whose mother never spoke to my mother.

The diary sputters intermittently through August and September, my father noting only "the rest of September spent gardening, studying and on the river in the afternoon." On October 11 he is off to London again to complete his examinations. They are "stiff," but he passes and is now an associate member of the Institute of Civil Engineers. He spends two shillings to hear Harry Lauder at the Tivoli, but the diary becomes blank for a few pages, marked only with the names "London and Esperson"—and suddenly it is December 5. For a few days Nellie seems to accept him again. He presents her with a bouquet of violets which she wears in her coat; he feels like throwing his cap in the air he is so happy and he thanks God for all His mercies. Violets? It is the second time he has done this. There was always something between my mother and father about violets, though I never quite understood it.

My father's hopes, however, are again shattered; the diary becomes sporadic and is full of disappointments. He has lost his vitality, his zest for life. There is a diary entry for 13 February 1911—followed by a gap of one year. It must have been an unhappy one; he made the decision to emigrate to Canada. There are faded photographs labelled "Montreal 1911" and "Toronto 1912"—and then the diary flickers weakly and briefly once more. On 12 May 1912 he records his departure from

Toronto for the west with Charlie Dobbs, and on the following day he describes the desolation of the country between Chapleau and White River. There is no more.

It has been nice getting to know my father.

I know he worked in Montreal in 1911 and in Toronto in 1912 and I know he was living in Burnaby in September 1912 when he received a letter signed by C. C. Worsfold appointing him draughtsman "during the pleasure of the Department." And I know he lived in Lingannoch on Ulster Street, and that he went overseas with the Canadian Engineers during the war. I learned, too, that Nellie Murdoch was engaged to a fellow who was killed in that war, and that my Grandmother Morton did not attend her son's wedding in Perth on 4 July 1919. My father never explained this strange behaviour. In the notes he made for my family history on his pink pad of paper he said only that none of the Mortons attended "out of respect to my mother only," but his Uncle David gave them a wedding gift and later invited them to the Muirton.

The convoluted cycle, I suppose, is complete: the life of a remarkable man who was known only marginally to the public, and the life of his ancestors. It is pleasing knowledge. And yet there are new cycles intertwined with the old; mine with my father's, my sons' with mine. There are still strong ties with Perth. My son, in his nineteeth year, reversed the pattern of emigration by his grandfather. He lives in Britain, visits Maymie Lindsay who was there in the days of the fourteen children of old John Morton and knew many of them. My son, on his holidays, has worked in the Lindsays' potato fields in sight of the Muirton where his ancestors toiled; indeed, he met an ancient gentleman who had worked on the Muirton in the days of Uncle David. And my son, bolder than his father, entered Gannochyfold and stood in my father's room where the present owner asked if the letter "K" meant anything to him. It was scratched into the window glass of my father's room.

Perhaps with successive generations the ties with Perth will weaken, fade and be forgotten. In 1976 the Muirton farmhouse was torn down and the land was covered by the ubiquitous housing development. Yet one can still find on the ground an old piece of slate tile from the farmhouse roof. Gannochyfold is still there—and you can stand on Balhousie Street at the very gate before which my mother and father stood in the tumultuous years of the diary and see the dimmed form of the name Dunearn fading from the stone above the doorway. The Morton stone still stands in Wellshill, its slender spire stark against the sky, placed there surely by one who wished to remember his family, or have it remembered.

And in my home there are mementoes of those distant years. There is an 1866 edition of the works of Byron in which is the bookplate of Perth Academy. On it is written, in a neat but shaky hand, "To James Morton for Chemistry, Practical Mathematics, Arithmetic, an Essay etc. Session 1866-67." My grandfather was seventeen years of age at the time, his youngest sister was not yet a year and his father, John of Forgandenny, was fifty-nine years. There is a silver biscuit barrel that my father's Uncle John won in 1882 for his crop of neeps, presented by A. & G. Cairncross, still a prominent goldsmith in the city of Perth. There is the woollen sweater my father's Uncle David brought from New Zealand in 1898, last washed and mended by Murdoch 2. There is a small pewter teapot engraved with the initials J. M. and the date Dec. 29, 1881, the wedding day of my paternal grandmother and grandfather.

There is silver from my grandmother's home—great silver gravy spoons and finely filigreed jam spoons and a silver spoon through which sugar sieves to sweeten strawberries. There is a toy steam engine which, when filled with water and placed over a spirit lamp, will steam and puff, and its brass fly-wheel, driven by its piston, will spin magnificently, as it did for my father when he was a child. My father's pencil box is on my desk and his rugby cap upon my bookcase. There is my father's silver-mounted cherrywood walking stick, a gift from Bob

Clark's mother on his twenty-first birthday—and my Uncle John's walking stick, which plodded the streets of Edinburgh beside me and stood straight between his legs as we sat on the bus or streetcar. There are Uncle John's war medals and my father's World War I name tag, announcing, for those who cared, that he was a Presbyterian. My eldest son has my father's gold watch, my younger son the gold watch that my Uncle John set so carefully to Big Ben's resonant chime at nine o'clock each evening as we sat talking in his flat on Comiston Road. And in my father's meagre papers there was a letter from my Uncle John written shortly after their mother's death in 1938. In it he says, in passing, that he is sending on some stamps their mother preserved for "the boys"—the collective term reserved for my brother and me. It touches a responsive spot in my heart. She had parted from her son under unpleasant circumstances and had never seen her three grandchildren.

There are two small plans of the Fraser drawn in the blackest India ink on grey-blue paper, with terms my father used— jetties and dykes and rockfills—in his strong, clear printing, which he had magically transposed from figures he pressed into his small brown surveyor's book in the wheelhouse of the *Samson*. And there are celluloid set squares and beautiful bone rulers delicately etched, pens holding nibs of all sizes and shapes, and protractors and compasses, and great heavy parallel rulers on little grooved rollers which still rumble if you roll them up my desk. My desk? It is as solid as the day my father made it, without a nail, forty years ago. It is difficult to escape my father in our home. You can write at his desk, read beneath his lamp or sit upon the fireplace boxes he formed from hammered copper. You can stand at the foot of the bed my father built from the wheel of the *Samson* and touch the spokes that Captain Jimmy Rogers once spun beneath the bridges of the Fraser.

I enjoy my artifacts. They are are not sad mementoes of happier days; they are merely inanimate objects that outlived the organisms who were my ancestors. They gave happiness in the past and they give happiness in the present.

The house on Fourteenth Avenue still stands, but only by the grace of the current housing developer who will one day stumble upon it. Along with the summerhouse my father built, it is in disrepair. The fruit trees he purchased from Mr. Living-stone near Central Park have grown wild, though my father's Transparent graft on the Delicious apple tree still survives. The tennis court is in ruins and the garden is overgrown. The cement paths he laid from the sand he dug are shattered with age, and the driveway is cluttered with weeds. It does not matter. It does not grieve me. There was achievement and pleasure there. The pillars at the foot of the driveway still stand as solidly as when my father built them from the granite rock he split so patiently fifty years ago. They will remain for as long as man will allow them to stand. But perhaps even more permanent is the great stone column in Wellshill and the echo of Prince Charles's feet tramping down the dusty road from Perth.